CHARLES DICKENS

Charles Dickens was born in Portsmouth in 1812. He studied at Wellington House Academy and worked as a law clerk, court stenographer and shorthand reporter, which led to his first collection of pieces, *Sketches by Boz* (1836).

His major works include *The Pickwick Papers* (1836), *Oliver Twist* (1837–9), *Nicholas Nickleby* (1838–9), *A Christmas Carol* (1843), *Martin Chuzzlewit* (1843–4), *David Copperfield* (1849–50), *Bleak House* (1852–3), *Hard Times* (1854), *Little Dorrit* (1855–7), *A Tale of Two Cities* (1859), *Great Expectations* (1860–1), *Our Mutual Friend* (1864–5) and the unfinished *The Mystery of Edwin Drood* (1870), as well as other novels, books and short stories. None of his major works has ever gone out of print.

Dickens married Catherine Hogarth in 1836 and had ten children with her. He died in June 1870 from a stroke and, contrary to his wish to be buried in Rochester Cathedral, was buried in Poet's Corner of Westminster Abbey.

PIERS TORDAY

Piers Torday began his career in theatre and then television as a producer and writer. As a producer, his credits include *Ben'n'Arn* (Perrier Comedy Award Best Newcomer), *The Dybbuk* (Battersea Arts Centre, James Menzies-Kitchin Memorial Award), *Resident Alien* and *Julie Burchill is Away* (Soho Theatre). His writing for TV includes *The Royals* (BBC America) and *Southside* (BBC Three). His first book for children, *The Last Wild*, was shortlisted for the Waterstones Children's Book Award and nominated for the CILIP Carnegie Medal. His second book, *The Dark Wild*, won the Guardian Children's Fiction Prize. *There May Be A Castle* was nominated for the CILIP Carnegie Medal, a People's Book Award finalist and a Times Children's Book of the Year. *The Lost Magician* was a Book of the Year in six national newspapers and won the Teach Primary Book Award. The follow up, *The Frozen Sea*, was published in 2019. Piers has also completed an unfinished novel by his late father Paul (author of *Salmon Fishing in the Yemen*), *The Death of an Owl*. His previous plays include *The Ripple Effect* (Pleasance Edinburgh) and his adaptation of John Masefield's *The Box of Delights* (Wilton's Music Hall). Formerly a trustee of Rose Theatre Bankside and Pleasance Theatre Trust, he is now a trustee of The Unicorn Theatre, The Ministry of Stories and an Artistic Associate at Wilton's Music Hall.

Charles Dickens

CHRISTMAS CAROL

a fairy tale

adapted for the stage by

Piers Torday

NICK HERN BOOKS

London

www.nickhernbooks.co.uk

A Nick Hern Book

Christmas Carol – a fairy tale first published as a paperback original in Great Britain in 2019 by Nick Hern Books Limited, The Glasshouse, 49a Goldhawk Road, London W12 8QP, in association with Wilton's Music Hall, London

Christmas Carol – a fairy tale copyright © 2019 Piers Torday

Piers Torday has asserted his right to be identified as the author of this version

Cover image: Design by Donovan Graphics. Photograph of Sally Dexter by Nobby Clark

Designed and typeset by Nick Hern Books, London
Printed in Great Britain by Mimeo Ltd, Huntingdon, Cambridgeshire PE29 6XX

A CIP catalogue record for this book is available from the British Library

ISBN   978 1 84842 914 7

Woodland
CARBON
www.woodlandcarbon.co.uk
NICK HERN BOOKS
Printed on Carbon Captured paper

Christmas Carol – a fairy tale was first performed at Wilton's Music Hall, London, on 29 November 2019, with the following cast:

FAN MARLEY (NÉE SCROOGE)	Sally Dexter
WANT/YOUNG FAN/SID FEZZIWIG, ANN CRATCHIT/GHOST OF CHRISTMAS FUTURE/ENSEMBLE	Chisara Agor
IGNORANCE/EBENEZER SCROOGE/ FRANK FEZZIWIG/TINY TIM/ NEVILLE/JOE/ENSEMBLE	Joseph Hardy
BOB CRATCHIT/BEAU FEZZIWIG/ GHOST OF CHRISTMAS PRESENT/ WILLIAM DORSET/FREDDIE SCROOGE/ ENSEMBLE	Edward Harrison
MR BULLABY/PRIEST/SCROOGE'S FATHER/FEZZIWIG/JACOB MARLEY/ TOPPER/BILL BULLABY/TURKEY/ ENSEMBLE	Brendan Hooper
FREDERICA/FROU-FROU/GHOST OF CHRISTMAS PAST/FIONA SCROOGE MRS DILBER/GHOST OF CHRISTMAS FUTURE/ENSEMBLE	Ruth Ollman
MEAGRE/POLL/CATHERINE FEZZIWIG/AMY DORSET/ALEXA/ ENSEMBLE	Yana Penrose
VOICE OF FRANCESCA SCROOGE	Asha Sylvestre

Director	Stephanie Street
Designer	Tom Piper
Lighting Designer	Katharine Williams
Composer and Sound Designer	Ed Lewis
Puppetry Designer	Jo Lakin
Movement and Puppetry Director	Emma Brunton
Casting Director	Gabrielle Dawes
Assistant Director	Josie Lena Davies

Producer	Holly Kendrick
Production Manager	Cath Bates
Stage Manager	Sophie Sierra

Costume Supervisor	Caroline Hughes
Wardrobe Mistress	Kat Day-Smith
Deputy Stage Manager	Emma Dymott
Puppet Maker	Stephanie Elgersma
Marketing and Sales Directors	EMG Marketing and Media Ltd
PR	Borkowski

Wilton's Music Hall

Executive Director | Holly Kendrick
General Manager | Anna Williams

Head of Development and Communications | Harry Hickmore
Marketing and Communications Manager | Lani Strange

Production Manager | Cath Bates
Technical and Facilities Manager | Ryan Funnell
Deputy Technical Manager | Jake Hughes
Technical and Facilities Assistant | Rye Milligan

Head of Commercial Services and Operations | Kate Mullan
Box Office and Reception Manager | Nathan Rumney
Venue Manager – Front of House and Customer Services |
Ellie Standeven
Venue Manager Bar and Commercial Services | Ross Bonny-Hodges
Bar Supervisor | Stephanie Colclough
Cleaners | John Thomas and Milka Krasteva

Heritage and Artistic Engagement Officer | Alice Cox

Front of House Team includes
Muireann Grealy, Gillian Howard, Amy Johnson, Sarah Lodge, Angela
Maasalu, Fatima Niemogha, Vanessa Quiney, Abida Ruma, Kerri
Sullivan and. Domokos Wootsch, Jess Millward, Anthony Gingell, Paul
Hutchinson, Kai Turner, Amelia Costello.

Box Office Team includes
Zhaleh Bahraini, Rupert Dannreuther, Alun Hood, Amy Johnson, Vanessa
Quiney, Jacqueline Busby, Ruth Carnegie, Grace Patrick, Sofia Sousa,
Christopher Spraggs, Gwenan Bain.

Bar Team
Chloe Astleford, Gwenan Bain, Simran Bhandari, Nathan D'Arcy, Kirsty
Greenhalgh, Richard Langford, Miki Lowe, Sarah Mercade, Sean
Murray, Eva Orupold, Sofia Sousa, Jodie Stempel, Simone Tropea,
Rebecca White, Olivia Williams, Christopher Spraggs, Esther Cameron,
Amelia Costello, Estelle Homerstone.

Press | Borkowski PR

Finance | Matthew Ashwood for Anstey Bond

Board of Trustees
George Marsh (Chair)
Dr John Gayner, Melanie Gurney, James Heaton, Kathleen Herron,
Andy Makin, Bill Taylor, Mark Tierney and Anne Vallely.

Wilton's Music Hall
for everyone with a curious imagination

'Wilton's is a nice place to visit. It does well-curated, intimate theatre and cabaret. But there's more to this fantastically atmospheric Victorian music hall. Wilton's is a palimpsest: there's a story about the shifting tides of London in its ravaged brickwork and wonky floors. It's a survivor, and proof that the spirit of London can be encapsulated in bricks and mortar. It also proves that Londoners will always want places to come together.'

Time Out, September 2018 Top 50 Iconic Places in London

Wilton's is of international significance as it is the only surviving Grand Music Hall in the world. Wilton's has been a Grade II* listed building since 1971 and is situated in a conservation area.

The Music Hall was built in 1858 by the entrepreneur John Wilton. John also procured The Prince of Denmark pub, otherwise, and still, known as The Mahogany Bar and adjoining houses. The building opened in 1859 to much acclaim with some of the great music hall stars, such as Champagne Charlie and Arthur Lloyd, regularly performing. Due to Wilton's proximity to the docks there was an international cast and audience alike.

In the 1880s fire regulations changed and the Music Hall closed as a music hall and was purchased by a Wesleyan Mission and used by them until the 1950s, during which time they:

Fed 2,000 people a day during the dockers' strike of 1889.

Housed the first Ethiopian working men's club in the 1920s.

Supported the East End Anti-fascists in the 1930s providing a safe haven during the Battle of Cable Street in 1936.

Ran free Sunday activities for local children and gave them free fruit.

Ran free cinema screenings for the local community.

Offered skills training in sewing, woodwork and literacy.

Offered shelter in World War I and World War II for the people of East London.

The Methodists departed in 1950 and the building fell into disrepair despite a failed restoration attempt in the 1980s, which actually left the building gutted and structurally dangerous.

In 2019 the picture has changed somewhat. In 2015 we completed a three-year Heritage Lottery Funded capital project, which has conserved the Hall, maintaining the beautiful barley twist columns and the handsome balcony. After the completion of work on the Hall, the houses were then restored, ensuring that Wilton's had more front-of-house and commercial space as well as dedicated learning facilities. The rooms now are made up of: The Mahogany Bar, The John Wilton Room (a heritage and exhibition space), The Cocktail Bar, The Champagne Charlie Room, The Study, and The Aldgate and Allhallows Learning and Participation Studio.

Wilton's mission is to sustain the East End building and its unique spirit with a programme of extraordinary theatre and music, made for all of London and everyone with a curious imagination. Our building is now open and accessible every weekday, with an affordable artistic programme running all year round which in the last year has included work by the English National Opera, Balletboyz and Watermill Theatre, to name but a few.

Wilton's has also offered a unique, historic setting to a number of extraordinary films, meaning not only has the building's historic splendour been shared with a much wider public, but the hires from such films have enabled Wilton's to continually subsidise our artistic and community programmes. Some of the films shot at Wilton's include *Bleak House*, *Chaplin*, *Dancing on the Edge*, *De-Lovely*, *Dorian Gray*, *Interview with the Vampire*, *The Vampire Chronicles*, *Kiss Kiss (Bang Bang)*, *Mr Selfridge*, *Muppets Most Wanted*, *Nicholas Nickleby*, *Penelope*, *Sherlock Holmes: A Game of Shadows*, *Suffragette*, *The Grave Matter of Notorious Serial Killers Burke and Hare*, *The Krays* and *The Importance of Being Ernest*.

Wilton's has always been an exceptional place for an audience to hear live music, but we have also built up a reputation for world-class musicians recording their music videos in the space, such as Marc Almond, Adam Ant, Billy Bragg, Kate Bush, The Coral, Bryan Ferry, Frankie Goes to Hollywood, Kelis, Kwabs, Laura Marling, Mumford and Sons, Paolo Nutini, Frank Turner and Wild Beasts. To celebrate our musical heritage in May 2020 Wilton's will be presenting a festival of emerging musical talent.

For more information about Wilton's Music Hall visit
wiltons.org.uk

Adapting *Christmas Carol* – Author's Note

When Charles Dickens published his 'little Christmas book' in 1843, it took just six weeks for the first adaptation to reach the stage. It played in London for more than forty nights before transferring to New York. In the year of publication alone, there were nine separate theatrical adaptations, including the first-ever musical version. Dickens himself was famous for his own public readings of the story, giving over 127 such recitals in England and America. And the process of retelling has continued for 176 years. From stage to screen, cartoon to musical, from the RSC to the Muppets, there are nearly thirty published adaptations of *A Christmas Carol*, and dozens more are written every Christmas. There was even a mime version by Marcel Marceau in 1973.

So why another? Well, whilst the tale has been retold for puppets and toys, and Scrooge performed by men young and old, the central role has remained resolutely masculine. What happens when we re-examine this classic fairy tale from a woman's perspective, and reimagine the complex central character? And why?

The book is, at heart, a story about injustice. Dickens was horrified by the desperate destitution, especially in children, that he witnessed on his many legendary walks through industrial London. He initially drafted a political pamphlet in reply to an 1843 parliamentary report on working-class child poverty. But the *Carol* made his point more plangently.

Yet he was also no saint. It is perhaps telling that Catherine, his long-suffering wife (who was also a writer), titled her sole publication *What Shall We Have for Dinner?* She endured twelve pregnancies, bearing him ten children. These took their toll on her body, about which Dickens was privately offensive, and on her mind. Catherine was afflicted by what appears to have been severe post-natal depression, and Dickens responded by first taking up with a young actress, Ellen Ternan, then trying to persuade a doctor that his wife was insane, and should be put away in an asylum so he could continue his philandering unhindered.

Charles Dickens's daughter Katey said that her father never understood women, and some of his excessively sentimentalised young female characters, like Little Nell in the *Old Curiosity Shop*, or the long parade of unattractive or damaged older women, such as Miss Havisham in *Great Expectations*, do not offer a very compelling counterargument to this analysis. But he was also a product of his age, a time of unstinting male power that frequently marginalised the voices of the poor, the indebted, the weak, the vulnerable – and women of all classes.

Christmas Carol is set in an intensely patriarchal society. The most powerful member of it, Queen Victoria, may have been a woman, but she also thought her own sex 'poor and feeble', and called for suffragists to be whipped. Her female subjects were expected to put 'home and hearth' before all else (often including any education and professional advancement). When she married, the rights of a woman were legally given to her husband. He took control of her property, earnings and money. If he wished to spend her money on his business or his debts, he did not require her consent. In exchange for this, she took his name. And until the 1857 Matrimonial Causes Act, divorce allowing remarriage was only possible by the passage of a private act through the Houses of Parliament.

Early nineteenth-century daughters, like the Fan Scrooge that Dickens imagines, were meant to get in line behind their brothers, like Ebenezer. In Dickens's version, Fan dies early, leaving Ebenezer distraught.

But what if it had been the other way around? What if Fan Scrooge had tried to make her way in a man's world of power and profit? What would have happened to Fan then?

Dickens wrote this enduring and uplifting story to try to heal the divisions of his own age. He yearned to create 'a better common understanding among those whose interests are identical and who depend upon each other'. He wanted, in other words, to bring all people together, at a precious time of year, united in a love of the common good. And so do we. Merry Christmas, and God bless us, *every one*.

Piers Torday
November 2019

Characters

NARRATORS
MEAGRE, *a Dickensian cat*
IGNORANCE, *a child of the streets*
WANT, *his sister*

THE SCROOGE FAMILY
FAN MARLEY (*née* SCROOGE), *a moneylender*
JACOB MARLEY, *her late husband*
FREDERICA, *her niece*
NEVILLE, *Frederica's husband*
TOPPER, *a family friend*
FATHER SCROOGE
EBENEZER SCROOGE, *her late brother*
YOUNG FAN SCROOGE
FIONA SCROOGE, *her great-great-great-granddaughter*
FRANCESCA SCROOGE, *her great-great-great-great-granddaughter*
FREDDIE SCROOGE, *her great-great-great-great-nephew*

THE CRATCHITS
BOB CRATCHIT, *Scrooge's clerk*
MRS ANN CRATCHIT, *his wife*
TINY TIM, *their invalid son*

THE SPIRITS
THE GHOST OF CHRISTMAS PAST
THE GHOST OF CHRISTMAS PRESENT
THE GHOST OF CHRISTMAS FUTURE

THE FEZZIWIGS
OLD FEZZIWIG, *a draper*
BEAU FEZZIWIG, *his son*
CATHERINE FEZZIWIG, *Beau's wife*
FRANK *and* SID FEZZIWIG, *their sons*

OTHERS
MR BULLABY, *an evangelical fundraiser*
BILL BULLABY, *his 2019 descendant*
MRS DILBER, *a pawnbroker*
JOE, *a thief*
WILLIAM DORSET, *a client of Scrooge's*
AMY DORSET, *his daughter*

NON-HUMANS
FROU-FROU, *a lapdog*
POLL, *a toy parrot*
A TURKEY
ALEXA

This text went to press before the end of rehearsals and so may differ slightly from the play as performed.

ACT ONE

Scene One

London, 1838. There is a bell that hangs above us all. In heavy fog, it tolls the funeral march.

A Dickensian cat of books and paper and ink, MEAGRE, *our narrator, appears out of the gloom. We see a boy,* IGNORANCE *and his sister,* WANT, *digging a hole for a coffin.*

MEAGRE. Good evening, friends... I have long wished to have the great pleasure of meeting you face to face, this Christmas time. Are we sitting comfortably?

The CHILDREN *notice him.*

IGNORANCE. Sister, did that cat just say something?

WANT. I don't want to say yes, but... yes, I think it did.

IGNORANCE (*to* MEAGRE). Who are you?

MEAGRE. Charles Dickens.

WANT. Charles Dickens? The author?

MEAGRE. Er... yes?

IGNORANCE. Look, I may not be able to read, but I'm pretty sure Charles Dickens wasn't a flaming cat!

MEAGRE. Aha! But maybe I was his cat!

WANT. So what if you were? You don't get every stray mutt standing up on stage saying here, you lot, guess what? I was Shakespeare's dog, now watch my Hamlet.

MEAGRE. I'm not here for him. I'm here for you.

IGNORANCE. For us? Why?

MEAGRE. To help you tell your story.

WANT. I want to know your name first.

MEAGRE. I told you, I'm Charles –

WANT. Your *real* name, cat.

MEAGRE. Very well… I'm called Meagre.

IGNORANCE. Do you know who we are? Cos I 'aven't a clue, mate.

MEAGRE. You'll find that out later.

WANT. I've wanted to know that for so long… Well, go on then.

MEAGRE. Thank you… Marley was dead! To begin with!

WANT. Jacob Marley? I wonder who he was.

IGNORANCE. Never 'eard of 'im.

They keep digging and then hammer a lid on to the coffin.

WANT. He is definitely dead, right?

MEAGRE. How could it have been otherwise? There is no doubt that Jacob Marley was dead.

IGNORANCE. As a doornail!

They lower the coffin into the ground, as an intoning PRIEST *emerges out of the gloom, followed by a veiled woman in black,* MRS FAN MARLEY (*née* SCROOGE).

PRIEST. I am the resurrection and the life, sayeth the Lord…

The CHILDREN *are impatient to get on.*

(*Flicking through prayer book.*) For as much as it hath pleased Almighty God, et cetera et cetera… to take out of this world the soul of our deceased brother Jacob Marley –

The CHILDREN *are really impatient. The* PRIEST *takes a swig from a hip flask.*

And so on till… ashes to ashes, dust to dust… (*Breaks off, holding out a handful of soil.*) Is there no one here who will mourn this man? Who will cast this earth? Anyone?

MRS MARLEY. For God's sake. I'll do it!

She steps out of the fog, with her umbrella.

PRIEST. And you are –

MRS MARLEY. His wife, for too many years. His sole executor, his sole beneficiary and – obviously, his only mourner. Now give me that. (*Takes the soil.*) Is it extra? No? Very well then. (*Cursorily scatters it.*) Is it over?

PRIEST. Have you nothing else to say?

MRS MARLEY. Humbug!

PRIEST. Mrs Marley! It's Christmas Eve!

MRS MARLEY. Humbug to Christmas Eve. Humbug to your robes and your false pieties, sir. Humbug to all weak men, and most of all, humbug to him! Jacob Marley! That scoundrel there took my liberty, my money and my property – such benefits which I paid for with the loss of my name. Before I became 'Mrs Marley', I had the name my father gave me, by which I shall once more live, and thrive as all women were born to do.

PRIEST. What name was that?

MRS MARLEY (*ripping off veil*). Scrooge!

The COMPANY *cheerfully create* SCROOGE *and* MARLEY*'s warehouse over the grave while the* NARRATORS *sing their story song, which we shall return to.*

IGNORANCE (*sings*). I love to tell the story
    For those who know it best
    Seem hungering and thirsting
    To hear it like the rest!

WANT. I love to tell the story
    Because I know 'tis true

It satisfies my longings
As nothing else can do.

COMPANY. And when in scenes of glory
We sing the new, new song
'Twill be the old, old story
That we have loved so long!
'Twill be the old, old story
That we have loved so long!

Scene Two

Seven years later.

The great bell tolls three o'clock in the afternoon, as
IGNORANCE *and* WANT *sit begging with* MEAGRE.

*There is a fog everywhere and the sound of dogs barking in the
street, carts clattering…*

WANT. Scrooge painted out Old Marley's name above the door.

IGNORANCE. Why'd she do that then?

WANT. Because she took his business over, didn't she? She
needed the money to live! Like we all do.

MEAGRE. She was a tight-fisted hand at the grindstone, hard
and sharp as flint. A squeezing, wrenching, grasping,
covetous old sinner.

IGNORANCE. Yer what?

WANT. He means she was a right greedy old b–

MEAGRE. Her cold heart froze her features, sharpened her
pointed nose, turned her lips blue, and even snow wouldn't
melt on her. Until, one dark and wintry Christmas Eve, seven
years later…

WANT *holds out a hat to* SCROOGE, *who knocks it back
with her umbrella as she enters her counting house.*

BOB CRATCHIT, *her clerk, is buried deep in a small red book.*

CRATCHIT. Miss Scrooge!

SCROOGE. Did I say you could light that fire?

CRATCHIT. No, but old Mr Marley, on a cold winter night such as this, he thought nothing of –

SCROOGE. Old Mr Marley is dead, and has been for seven years. Put it out please. I'm not made of money. (*Beat.*) Or I will put you out!

There is a loud hammering at the door. SCROOGE *flings it open.*

Oh God.

There is a young lady in a bonnet, SCROOGE'*s niece* FREDERICA, *with her lapdog,* FROU-FROU.

FREDERICA (*sings*). We wish you a Merry Christmas – Aunt Scrooge!
We wish you a Merry Christmas – Aunt Scrooge!
We wish you a Merry Christmas –

FROU-FROU. And a Happy New Year!

SCROOGE. Whatever you're selling, I'm not interested.

She slams the door in FREDERICA'*s face.*

FROU-FROU. She was so heated from walking in the frost and the fog, that she was all aglow, this niece of Scrooge's, her face flushed and pretty. But this was also because she had to carry me. I never walk anywhere!

FREDERICA. Aunt Scrooge! It's your niece Frederica! I'm not selling anything.

SCROOGE (*opening door*). Perhaps you should be. You're poor enough. (*Slams door again.*)

FREDERICA. Don't be cross, Aunt! You are rich enough, and it is Christmas!

SCROOGE *opens the door.*

SCROOGE. That's exactly why I'm not letting you in.

FREDERICA. I only want to invite you to dinner, sweet Aunt.

SCROOGE. It gets worse.

FREDERICA. Do not be so angry, I pray you, oh sweet Aunt.

SCROOGE. What else can I be, when I live in such a world of foolish women as you? Out upon Merry Christmas! (*Aside*.) What's Christmas time to women but a time for paying bills without money, spending money that is not yours on candles and trees! If I could work my will, every woman who goes about with 'Merry Christmas' on her lips should be boiled alive with her own pudding!

FREDERICA. Oh, Aunt. Oh, sweet Aunt. I always thought Christmas a good time, a kind time, a charitable time –

FROU-FROU. A yum-yum time! A massive-pile-of-presents time!

SCROOGE. A waste of time!

FREDERICA. – the only time, good Aunt, that I know of when men *and* women seem by consent to open their shut-up hearts freely!

SCROOGE. Men seem all too content to open their hearts freely all year round. Whether we ask for it or not.

FREDERICA. I only wished to invite you to dinner!

SCROOGE. To dinner! Why do you make such work for yourself, with not a penny to be earned for it? Why on earth did you ever get married?

FREDERICA. Because I fell in love!

FROU-FROU. It's such a beautiful story, I should tell you some time.

SCROOGE. Bah! Love? Fairy tales are for children. A good afternoon to you.

FREDERICA. A Merry Christmas to you, Aunt.

SCROOGE (*showing her out*). *Good afternoon.*

FROU-FROU. And a Happy New Year! Aunt!

> SCROOGE *is left alone with* CRATCHIT *once more.*

SCROOGE (*mutters*). 'Merry Christmas, Aunt!' 'Happy New Year, Aunt!'

> *Another knock.*

> The season of peace! If only I was to ever get any. (*To door.*) What now?

> *She flings it open, and* MR BULLABY *sweeps past in his coat, sweeping papers off desks.*

MR BULLABY (*to* CRATCHIT). Mr Marley, I presume? Or is it Mr Scrooge?

SCROOGE. Neither. Mr Marley died seven years ago today, thank the Lord. I am Miss Scrooge, his widow.

MR BULLABY. Dear me. A female of the species! And a moneylender! How charmingly unconventional. Mr Bullaby, at your service.

SCROOGE. Can I help, Mr Bullaby? Or are you just going to stand there and knock things off my desk all afternoon?

MR BULLABY. I hope you can help, Miss Scrooge, for I have come to spread the word.

SCROOGE. Not to mention your coat. What word... let me guess? Is it *Christmas*?

MR BULLABY. Charity, Miss Scrooge! Christian charity.

SCROOGE. Oh, good. My second-least favourite word in the English language.

MR BULLABY. Why, what is the first?

SCROOGE. Christmas.

MR BULLABY. My dear lady, this is so regrettably different to... others of this parish, many of whom have given most liberally to this cause.

SCROOGE. I am sure they have. But my late husband left me with nothing other than this business, and I must work every hour daylight brings to survive.

MR BULLABY. It is my unenviable task to inform you, that not all your sex are as upstanding and virtuous as you. Like generations of men before me, I feel compelled to save these poor women from themselves.

SCROOGE. No doubt. How, exactly?

MR BULLABY. Education! Mr Bullaby's School for Fallen Young Ladies is a port in a storm for the wayward, the poor, even the criminal. We teach them the Christian virtues of a happy home, and turn young sinners into angels of the humble hearth, a credit to their future husbands and families.

SCROOGE. Are there no prisons?

MR BULLABY. Plenty, but Miss Scrooge –

SCROOGE. And the union workhouses? Are they in full operation?

MR BULLABY. They are still, but we are trying to provide an alternative –

SCROOGE. The treadmill and the Poor Law, they are both in good order, are they?

MR BULLABY. They have never worked better, I fear.

SCROOGE. Well, that is a relief. Let them go to prison! And to the workhouses! (*Aside.*) For it is only there that they may learn the truth of their existence in this world, and perhaps how to fight for themselves.

MR BULLABY. Many cannot go there, and many that do, die. Have you no charity in your heart?

SCROOGE. My heart is no concern of yours, and never was. Good day to you!

MR BULLABY. May I not even put you down for a penny?

SCROOGE. Not even one. And if you stay a second longer, I will start billing you for my time. Good day, sir!

She ushers MR BULLABY *out.*

CRATCHIT. Miss Scrooge, I –

SCROOGE. How are we doing with Mr Dorset? Has he paid yet?

CRATCHIT. He promises by the 28th.

SCROOGE. He promises, he always promises… Prepare the necessary papers.

CRATCHIT. But he has just lost his wife… he has funeral expenses…

SCROOGE. I lost my husband some seven years ago. And look at me now! He should consider it a blessing. The independent human, unencumbered by dependents, sails forth into the world, free to devote their life to the true gods of this age.

CRATCHIT. And what are they?

SCROOGE. Power and profit, Cratchit. For by what other means are we to make anything of ourselves?

CRATCHIT. She leaves behind three children… it is Christmas…

SCROOGE. I am well aware of the season, Mr Cratchit. Are the laws of the country suspended?

CRATCHIT. Of course not –

SCROOGE. Has all debt been forgiven for eternity?

CRATCHIT. No, but –

SCROOGE. Very well then. Papers.

CRATCHIT *reluctantly binds a pile of documents with ribbon, and then –*

CRATCHIT. They are done. Miss Scrooge, there was one other thing –

SCROOGE. Now what! You'll be wanting all day off tomorrow too, I suppose?

CRATCHIT. If it's convenient.

SCROOGE. It is not convenient and it is not fair. Will Mrs Cratchit be taking Christmas Day off too?

CRATCHIT. Yes, the milliner's will be shut for the day. Hat-making is such hard work, her hands –

SCROOGE. And how will she be enjoying this precious free day? Sitting in front of the fire, reading a volume of light verse with her feet up while you drop sugar plums into her mouth?

CRATCHIT. No – she has the laundry, then we have a small goose to roast and then there is Tiny Tim too, he needs extra care of course…

SCROOGE. You must have the day off, I see, while Mrs Cratchit washes and feeds you all, just as she does every day of the year, on top of her job at the hat factory. She works extra for nothing, while I pay you extra to *do* nothing.

CRATCHIT. It is the custom… but once a year…

SCROOGE. Which is once too many! I have little choice, I suppose. But you had better be early the day after, to make up for lost time.

CRATCHIT. Yes, ma'am… There was one other thing… another custom… I trust you don't object.

He hands SCROOGE *a small present.*

SCROOGE. Cratchit! You shouldn't have.

CRATCHIT. It's my pleasure.

SCROOGE. No, really, you shouldn't have. I haven't got anything for you.

CRATCHIT. That's no matter, ma'am. I thought you… might find it of interest.

SCROOGE, *unsure at first, tears the present open.*

A book.

SCROOGE (*peering over glasses*). *The Condition of the Working Class in England* by Frederick Engels. Awful title. I do not care for humorous novels.

CRATCHIT. It is neither humorous, nor a novel… I do wish you would read it. Ma'am, it has given me cause to reflect upon our business, Miss Scrooge.

SCROOGE. I trust Mr Engels approves.

CRATCHIT. He does not! We… make money out of money!

SCROOGE. A shrewd fellow. Is he looking for a job?

CRATCHIT. We trap those without money in a perpetual cycle of debt, keeping the ownership of capital forever out of the hands of the working man –

SCROOGE. The more you talk of the working man, the more I am inclined to decrease their ranks by one number.

CRATCHIT. I wish you could see, Miss Scrooge, with your own eyes, what is happening to this country. People sleeping on the streets, the hungry dependent on parcels of food from the charitable, children going to school without clothes and meals –

SCROOGE. Good evening, Cratchit.

CRATCHIT. Merry Christmas, Miss Scrooge.

The clock strikes six.

CRATCHIT *hurriedly clears up his desk and clears off out into the fog, scarf trailing.*

SCROOGE *tries to return to work but it is no good.* CRATCHIT *has unsettled her. And then – another knock. She opens the door, looking out above their heads.*

IGNORANCE, WANT *and* MEAGRE *are at her door, this time singing a carol, with a hat for collections.*

IGNORANCE, WANT *and* MEAGRE (*superfast*).
  God rest ye merry gentlemen
  Let nothing you dismay
  Remember Christ our Saviour
  Was born on Christmas Day
  To save us all from Satan's pow'r
  When we were gone astray
  Oh tidings of comfort and joy
  Comfort and joy
  Oh tidings of comfort and joy!

SCROOGE. Hello? Curious. I could have sworn I heard a really irritating noise.

She slams the door shut on them.

The carol continues in a creepy, instrumental echo as SCROOGE *locks up her counting house and makes her way home through the evening fog, which seems to deepen and thicken as she goes.*

There is another sound now too – faint at first… of chains scraping.

She turns around. But there is nothing there.

Yet still they scrape…

Scene Three

The gloomy entrance to SCROOGE*'s rooms.*

IGNORANCE *and* WANT *watch with* MEAGRE *as she fumbles with the lock.*

IGNORANCE. What a gloomy old dump. What's she doing there?

WANT. She lives there. I wish I had somewhere to live.

MEAGRE. It was old enough, and gloomy enough, for nobody lived in it but Scrooge.

IGNORANCE. The narrow street was so dark that she had to grope with her hands to find her way.

WANT. Not a yard you would ever want to be lost in.

MEAGRE. And when she at last found her own dwelling, fog and frost so hung about the black old doorway, that she almost –

SCROOGE (*screams*). Marley!

A pale, grinning, worm-eaten skull where the door knocker was, laughing at her –

Then she looks again – just a door knocker.

SCROOGE *shakes her head and hurriedly lets herself in.*

It is pitch black inside. Fumbling, she finds herself a candle, locks the door behind her.

IGNORANCE. I don't see what she's so scared of.

MEAGRE. Scrooge was not a woman to be frightened easily. But she locked, and double-locked herself in –

IGNORANCE. She checked her rooms, under the bed, behind the sofa. Dunno why. Nothing there, was there?

MEAGRE. There was only a low fire in the grate, with just a tiny saucepan of gruel.

WANT. I could kill for some gruel.

MEAGRE. And then –

The door swings open with a loud creak, blowing out the candle.

No one there but the fog, swirling in. She shuts and double-locks the door.

SCROOGE. Humbug!

She returns to her gruel and relights the candle. The bell above begins to ring, slowly at first.

This isn't happening!

Ringing crazily now, no rhythm, fit to wake the dead –

SCROOGE *grabs at the bell pull and yanks. With a sudden rush of chains, the pull comes clattering down. And out of this pile emerges* MARLEY, *wrapped and laden in them.*

Jacob Marley!

MARLEY. My wife!

SCROOGE. Good of you to drop in.

MARLEY. I am the spirit that once was!

SCROOGE. You're chained.

MARLEY. When living, it was required that I should walk forth amongst my fellow men, far and wide, but I did not.

SCROOGE. You can say that again. You barely left the sofa.

MARLEY. Hence I am now doomed to wander through the world after death.

SCROOGE. Thanks for explaining to me what a ghost is…

MARLEY. You doubt your own senses, wife?

SCROOGE. It's my stomach playing tricks. You may be an undigested bit of beef, a blot of mustard, a fragment of underdone potato – there's more of gravy than the grave about you!

MARLEY. Glad to see you still have your famous sense of
humour...

SCROOGE. What do you want?

MARLEY. Much!

SCROOGE. Same here. I'll start, then. Jacob – I want
a divorce.

MARLEY. But I'm dead!

SCROOGE. Yet here you still are, moaning on as before, so –

MARLEY. Were we not happy?

SCROOGE. *You* were happy.

MARLEY. But I gave you everything! My business, my name –

SCROOGE. No, you *took* everything! My name, my money, my
liberty.

MARLEY. As was my right.

SCROOGE. Was it also your right to be faithless? Was it your
right to use what little money I had, inherited from my
brother Ebenezer, to pay off your debts?

MARLEY. I loaned you money when you had none, on very
generous terms. I gave you a roof over your head, food –
I paid for you. I owned you. And now you repay that
generosity with divorce?

SCROOGE. Perceptive as ever.

MARLEY. Impossible! It requires an Act of Parliament –

SCROOGE. There you have it. The chains of custom bind us
for life, and even beyond the grave it seems...

MARLEY. I wear only *these* chains, the ones I forged in life.
I made them link by link, yard by yard, in the operation of
my business without compassion or charity, when mankind
should have been my business!

SCROOGE. With scarce a thought for womankind?

MARLEY. You are right. The common welfare of *all* should have been my business. Let us say humankind. Including you, dear wife – which is the reason I'm here.

SCROOGE. I knew it. You want something. Only ever nice when you wanted something.

MARLEY. I want you to show charity, forbearance, and benevolence! As I should have, not least to you, and in doing so, forged these chains. You now risk the same fate. Promise me you will change.

SCROOGE. You promised me love. But you took everything I owned and betrayed my trust. All I am doing now is reclaiming what should have been mine.

MARLEY. At what cost? Please listen to me. I know I did you ill. Many times. It pains me to see that you have no more love in your heart. You are not the woman I first knew. If I am to blame for this, then add another hundred yards to my chains, and then a hundred more. I come to save you!

SCROOGE. I do not need to be saved by anyone, least of all my dead husband.

MARLEY. Nevertheless. You will be haunted by three spirits – until you change. Expect the first tomorrow morning, when the bell tolls one.

SCROOGE. Can't I have all three at once? I'm rather busy.

MARLEY. Expect the second an hour later! And the third an hour after that, on the last stroke of three!

SCROOGE. And how about you? We have unfinished business.

MARLEY. Look to see me no more!

SCROOGE. Will I be free of you forever?

MARLEY. See me no more! See me no more!

SCROOGE. Promises, promises...

MARLEY. They come tonight!

MARLEY *disappears, his ghostly final words echoing around, over and over, while* SCROOGE *prepares for bed – setting her candle down by the floor, hanging up her dressing gown on the bedpost…*

Scene Four

The ghostly echoes are dispersed abruptly by the bell striking one.

Everything is pitch black.

We can just make out SCROOGE *sleeping fitfully.*

Something runs across the stage, we can't see what, a patter of feet.

SCROOGE. Hello?

Then the thing moves fast again – a blur of light!

Is someone there?

A faint peal of childish laughter.

Who is that?

Feet pattering. SCROOGE *fumbles for the candle by her bed, lights it.*

Cautiously looks this way, that way, the room is empty, and then –

A flash of a child's face in her candle flame.

Then it's gone again.

What trickery is this?

Show yourself.

I said show yourself!

It appears again, a childish face lit by a candle.

PAST (*childish*). Hello.

SCROOGE. Now, listen, if this is some kind of jest –

It vanishes and appears elsewhere.

PAST. Hello, Fan.

SCROOGE. I must still be dreaming.

PAST. Come and play with me, Fan.

SCROOGE. No. Get out of my mind. I must get back to sleep.

PAST. Play with me, Fan.

SCROOGE. Play with you? What?

PAST. In the past.

SCROOGE. Who are you?

PAST. The spirit whose coming was foretold to you. A Ghost of
Christmas Past. Rise and walk with me!

The bed curtains fall.

MEAGRE. As these words were spoken, they passed right
through the bedroom wall –

IGNORANCE. How'd they do that then?

WANT. It's a ghost, innit? They can walk through walls. I wish
I could walk through walls.

IGNORANCE. You're thin enough!

MEAGRE. They stood instead in an open country road, with
fields on either hand.

IGNORANCE. Oi! Where's London gone?

MEAGRE. The city had entirely vanished, the darkness and
mist with it, for it was a cold and clear day, with snow on the
ground.

WANT (*to* IGNORANCE). I am so cold, brother. Will you
hold me?

He does, and then they melt away, like the snow.

SCROOGE. I recognise this place. I was a girl here!

GHOST. You remember the way?

As they travel into the past, we hear CHILDREN *singing and playing faintly in the distance.*

CHILDREN (*sings*). Christmas is coming,
The geese are getting fat,
Please put a penny
In the old man's hat!

SCROOGE. I recognise those sounds, those voices –

PAST. What you see and hear are but shadows of things that have been.

MEAGRE. They left the road by a well-remembered lane to a house of dull red brick. It was a large building but one of broken fortunes – the walls damp, the windows cracked and in every poorly furnished room, an air of melancholy.

SCROOGE. My childhood home! It looks dark and deserted.

PAST. I can see something in the dark. Some*one*.

Her child self, FAN SCROOGE, *appears all alone.*

SCROOGE. My brother was sent away to school... I stayed at home.

PAST. Don't be sad, Fan.

SCROOGE. I had tried to forget all this... it was a long time ago. I have changed.

PAST. So much that you have forgotten who you were?

The child FAN *starts reading her book,* Robinson Crusoe.

SCROOGE. *Robinson Crusoe*! My favourite book... I read it to myself over and over again –

FAN (*reading aloud*). 'I dreamed that someone spoke to me, calling "Poor Robinson Crusoe! Where are you? Where have you been?" But I knew it was my parrot, Poll, and indeed it could be nobody else, for on this island, I was all alone.'

She picks up POLL, *a parrot toy, who transforms in her hands into a real talking parrot.*

POLL. Robinson Crusoe, where have you been? Robinson Crusoe!

FAN. Poll! You're really here. Where did you come from? I thought you were only in this book.

POLL. Where did you come from?

FAN. I have always been here, or at least so it feels like. My mother is lost to us. Now my father is always away at the tavern, my brother away at school.

PARROT. Away! Christmas! Away! Away!

FAN. Can you really talk, Poll, or do you just repeat what I say?

POLL. Just repeat what you say!

FAN. Why, you are a lot of humbug, you silly parrot!

POLL. *You* are a silly humbug!

FAN. Silly parrot!

POLL. Humbug!

They laugh together.

FAN (*sadly*). But are you here though, Poll, or am I just imagining a voice, like Robinson Crusoe in this story?

POLL. Just imagining!

FAN. I feared as much. That makes me so very sad. For you see, Poll, it is Christmas. Can you hear the other children, in the street, calling out 'Merry Christmas' to each other, as they return from school to their warm homes, and families…?

But she is all alone – the parrot has become a lifeless toy again.

Poll?

She clutches the parrot to her.

Merry Christmas, Poll. (*In* POLL *voice.*) Merry Christmas, Fan!

SCROOGE. Oh dear.

PAST. You sound sad. Don't be sad. Would you like to play in another Christmas instead?

SCROOGE. No, one was quite enough –

But PAST *waves her light, and now* FAN *is alone again, but playing 'The Ditchling Carol' on her piano,* POLL *watching.*

FAN (*sings*). Be merry all, be merry all
With holly dress the festive hall,
Prepare the song, the feast, the ball
To welcome merry Christmas
And oh! remember gentles gay,
For you who bask in fortune's ray,
The year is all a holiday –

A young boy bursts in, trailing a scarf, and a bag –

EBENEZER (*joining in with song*). 'The poor have only Christmas!'

FAN. Ebenezer! You came home!

EBENEZER. I could not bear to spend another Christmas without you, dear sister.

FAN. But Father –

EBENEZER. Oh, Father will be all right, little Fan. My schoolmaster wrote to him and told him it would be extra if I stayed over the holidays this year! That changed his mind quick enough.

FAN. You really mean it! You are not a ghost, then?

EBENEZER. I can confirm – I am not a ghost!

They embrace. It has been months.

FAN. I am glad of it. He drinks, brother. There is no money. He has such rages; I do not know –

EBENEZER. Not another word, sister! I am here now and all will be well. (*Sees* POLL.) What's this? Has Poll not left his desert island yet?

FAN. He has decided that I should stay. We are both growing used to the peace and quiet.

EBENEZER. Too much peace, I reckon.

FAN (*changing the subject*). Tell me, dear brother, about your school... what you do there...

EBENEZER. So much, dear sister. I read and read, and then there are sums, and studying maps, and playing with my fellows, and all the while, dreaming of –

FAN. Of home?

EBENEZER. Home? Er, of course, quite so, but also visions of the world ahead, what I shall do when I am older. Ideas, businesses, propositions... I am going to become quite the man of the town, dear sister, to make you proud. This family shall never be poor again!

FAN. And I, what am I to do?

EBENEZER. What do you mean?

FAN. What am I to do to make you proud, dear brother?

EBENEZER. You have your gift, do you not? (*Pats the piano.*) I have no doubt, dear sweet sister, that you are going to make the most wonderful music teacher.

FAN. Thank you for your faith, brother. That is a good and virtuous calling, only I have also had ideas –

EBENEZER. Or a governess? Or a wife? What does it matter? Come, I should not have put gloomy thoughts of the future into your head. I am home now, and I swear, my darling Fan, I shall never leave you again. Shall we always celebrate Christmas together?

FAN. You promise? No matter what happens, where life takes us, who we become –

EBENEZER. We'll always celebrate Christmas together!

FAN. And have the merriest, merriest time in all the world!

EBENEZER. Forever –

FAN. – and ever!

She sits at their piano and begins to play 'The Ditchling Carol' again.

As she plays, EBENEZER *joins her at the keyboard.*

SCROOGE. He was a blockhead, yet also as kind a brother as one could hope to have.

PAST. With a large heart.

SCROOGE. But a weak one… We lost him too young.

EBENEZER *fades into the shadows.*

PAST. I think he married. Did they have any babies?

SCROOGE. Yes, one. A girl.

PAST. That would make her your niece.

SCROOGE. I never got on with her mother, I'm afraid. Take me home, spirit, I've seen quite enough.

PAST. But there is another Christmas we can play in! Another!

She waves her light once more, and there is FAN *alone again, writing a letter.*

FAN. 'Dear brother, I wish Father would let you come back again this Christmas, like he did last year…'

She scrumples it up and tries again.

'Dear Ebenezer, it is lonely here without you, and Father's rages are – '

And again.

'Ebenezer, why is it me who must deal with everything? You are away in school, without a care in the world other than those of your studies and playmates, cares which I yearn for. I must watch as Father misses our mother, drinks, and falls further into debt. He cannot manage anything. I cook his meals, I darn his clothes, I mop the floor, and in return – '

A patriarchal shadow appears in the doorway.

FATHER. What are you doing, child?

FAN. I am… writing a letter, Father, to Ebenezer.

FATHER. Where did you find paper? And ink?

FAN. On your desk… in your study. Do not be angry with me, Father.

FATHER *(taking letter)*. This is my property! You have no business taking it. Your wretched mother died penniless. Now you both feed upon my beneficence, like leeches. The fees for Ebenezer's school take the most, and now I am to give you paper and ink too? This is what happens when a woman learns to read and write. Trouble!

He rips the letter up.

Do you not understand that if I cannot pay off these debts, I shall go to prison? Every penny counts, child. What shall you do if I am jailed? Let us hope there is a rich man out there foolish enough to take pity upon you and make you his wife.

FAN. But it was just a sheet of paper, Father –

FATHER. The price of which may well be my liberty! I shall teach you to rummage in my study without permission. Go and stand in the window there. Go on!

FAN. To do what?

FATHER. Wait! Until some other fool can take you off my hands. You cost enough as it is.

FAN. But, Father, it is Christmas –

FATHER. You will make a nice present for someone, I'm sure.

SCROOGE. Spirit, do not make me watch any more. I am too well aware of the forces that shaped me. But am I sad that I grew determined to overcome them, and make a place for myself against the odds? Never!

PAST. One more Christmas! Again!

SCROOGE. For the love of –

PAST. You will like it, I promise.

She waves her light once more. As MEAGRE *describes, so the scene moves on.*

MEAGRE. And in that moment, they left the family home behind them, and were now in the busy thoroughfares of a great city, where shadowy passengers passed and repassed, where carts and coaches battled for space.

IGNORANCE. That's more like it! The countryside is weird.

WANT. I like sheep, though. I want one. They're cuddly.

IGNORANCE. No one wants to cuddle us though. You'd better man up if you want to survive out here, sister.

MEAGRE. The streets were lighted up for Christmas time, and beneath their glare, they stopped at a certain warehouse door…

PAST. Have you been here before? Shall we play here?

SCROOGE. Can it possibly be…

PAST. Listen! They're dancing!

We hear the distant strains of a jig from inside. SCROOGE *recognises the tune.*

SCROOGE. Impossible! Do not torment me, spirit! I had put him out of my heart.

PAST. Who?

Scene Five

IGNORANCE *and* WANT *drag open the warehouse doors to reveal a dance in full swing.*

FEZZIWIG, *the spirit of Christmas cheer itself, in an enormous wig, stands on a chair, whooping and clapping.*

It's an after-work party, raucous and joyous.

A FIDDLER *plays on, underscoring the next exchange, while the dance continues in slow-motion silence –*

SCROOGE. Old Fezziwig!

PAST. What was he to you?

SCROOGE. My first employer… and yet so much more than that.

MEAGRE. Old Fezziwig was an organ of benevolence from the top of his wig to the tips of his shoes –

IGNORANCE. An organ of what?

WANT. It means he was a nice old gent who liked a laugh, a drink and a dance.

IGNORANCE. Well, why not just say that then? (*To* MEAGRE.) You're the most longwinded cat I ever met.

MEAGRE. His warehouse was as snug, and warm, and dry, and bright a ballroom as you would desire to see on a winter's night!

WANT. Oh, I am so cold, brother, I could just curl up and stay here, and sleep forever.

IGNORANCE. Don't sleep, sister, don't sleep. We need to keep moving. Come on – let's have a dance! (*Desperate.*) Come on!

He coaxes her into a little weary jig at the side of the action.

PAST (*to* SCROOGE). Now it is your turn to play!

SCROOGE. What? No – I don't dance any more –

PAST (*pushing her into the scene*). Go! See these shadows of your former self as they really were!

The party stops in fascination at the arrival of SCROOGE, *now as a bedraggled, shivering version of her younger self.*

FEZZIWIG. Yo-ho, young miss! Hilli-ho! What have we here?

SCROOGE. Please, sir, I am looking for work.

FEZZIWIG. On Christmas Eve! Poor child!

SCROOGE. My father has been sent to prison, he cannot pay his debts. We have no money.

FEZZIWIG. Hilli-ho, my lass, hilli-ho! What a business. But this is a warehouse.

SCROOGE. I have nowhere else to go. I saw the lights, heard the music… I am a competent seamstress –

FEZZIWIG. A seamstress! Yo-ho!

SCROOGE. You have a position? I have no references, I am afraid.

FEZZIWIG. We need no seamstress –

SCROOGE. Then I can clean, cook and launder too –

FEZZIWIG. Gadzooks!

SCROOGE. My father also says that I have a head for figures.

FEZZIWIG. Figures! Now you're talking.

SCROOGE. I kept the books for our household. Much good that it did me. Or him.

FEZZIWIG. Chirrup, lass! Not those figures. Can you do a figure of eight?

SCROOGE. I'm not sure –

FEZZIWIG. Then we'll show you how –

SCROOGE *gets whisked into the dance, passed around, reluctantly at first, then submitting to the spirit of the evening.*

(*To* BEAU.) Yo-ho, my lad! Show our guest. (*To* ALL.) That's the only kind of work we have tonight! Dance work! Well done! Well done, I say!

Faster and faster, until she is left with BEAU *for a round.*

A pause for breath.

BEAU. You've done this before.

SCROOGE. I've had plenty of time to practise. On my own.

BEAU. It's so typical of my father – not to even introduce us first! My name's Beau. Fezziwig.

SCROOGE. Fan. Scrooge.

BEAU. You are very welcome, Fan Scrooge!

SCROOGE. What is this place?

BEAU. A place of very great happiness.

SCROOGE. I have not known much happiness of late. What is the work you do?

BEAU. The usual. We buy, we sell. I am Mr Fezziwig's senior apprentice, as well as his son. We are all very thankful to work here. My father is the best master a man could hope for!

SCROOGE. He is very successful?

BEAU. He is better at throwing parties than counting the pennies, perhaps.

SCROOGE. My father taught me to count every penny…

BEAU. How is that working out for you?

SCROOGE. It's a sensible policy. If only he didn't drink so much. He is unhappy. After my mother –

BEAU. My father is quite insensible. Look at this madness! Half the year's profit will go on tonight. Yet he has the power to render us happy, or unhappy, to make our service a pleasure or a toil, and we are always happy, and it is always a pleasure. It's how he speaks to us and treats us. And you know the best thing about all of it?

SCROOGE. What?

BEAU. The happiness he gives is the greatest fortune he has.

SCROOGE. You can't be serious.

BEAU. On the contrary – it's priceless.

The scene freezes as the GHOST *hovers into view.*

IGNORANCE. Thank goodness for that. I thought they were going to fall in love for a moment.

WANT. I want to fall in love.

PAST. Do you want to stop playing now?

SCROOGE. No!

PAST. You think he's silly, I can tell.

SCROOGE. Who? Beau? No. I adored him.

PAST. Not him, the old one. Good at making people happy, less good at making money.

SCROOGE. He was of another age. It is not how I would choose to run a business. Very old fashioned, wasteful, not using modern working practices, a poor return for investors. (*Aside.*) But I know I do not make Cratchit happy in the same way. If I show him any kindness, in his eyes I will be weak, and then...

PAST. But what happened later that night? Play some more!

She waves her hand and the party disappears, apart from BEAU *and* SCROOGE, *and faint music and lights, off.*

BEAU. It's snowing.

SCROOGE. I don't want this to end.

BEAU. It needn't! Stay with us forever.

SCROOGE. But your father said there was no work.

BEAU. My father talks a lot of nonsense. Stay with us, Fan Scrooge. Stay with me.

SCROOGE. There is no position though –

BEAU. We do, in fact, have a vacancy.

SCROOGE. I am quite prepared to do anything to earn my keep.

BEAU. The demands of the role are very simple. A successful applicant will stay by my side at all times. They will have substantial experience in the matters of the heart.

SCROOGE. That was not the position I sought. My experience is limited at present.

BEAU. Limited but most relevant. Is it a role you might consider accepting?

SCROOGE. I don't know –

BEAU. By the light of this silver Christmas moon?

SCROOGE. Beau. We hardly know each other. I will stay but I must make myself useful too. I do not want to rely on charity. I could be an apprentice like you! Please let me be useful.

BEAU. You are useful, more useful than you know.

They embrace, dance and – freeze.

SCROOGE *steps out of the scene.*

SCROOGE. Only I wasn't useful. Not in the way he wanted.

PAST. He loved you.

SCROOGE. And I him! But…

PAST. You loved another too.

SCROOGE. That's an outrageous accusation, spirit. Even for a child-ghost… thing. Did Marley put you up to this? Take me home this instant. Now!

PAST. I didn't say it was a person… quick, hurry! We don't have much time. My light grows dim.

She waves her hand and the scene changes again as the party jig plays on in the distance, only now interwoven with the fractured chimes of time, bittersweet and elegiac.

Scene Six

The party has vanished, and we are alone with BEAU *and* FAN
in the warehouse, a year later.

MEAGRE. Scrooge became an apprentice alongside Beau,
learning his father's trade alongside him, and the pair drew
close, until, one year later –

IGNORANCE. I hope they're not going to kiss again. That was
gross.

WANT. You must be joking. I want them to get married. You
could be page boy and I could be bridesmaid!

BEAU *observes* FAN *buried already in a ledger, in the
warehouse office, candles burning low.*

BEAU. Fan. It is past nine in the evening. Christmas Eve!

FAN. These accounts will not reconcile themselves.

BEAU. But will they keep till the New Year?

FAN. There are also bills to be sent, creditors to be chased,
stock to be checked… am I missing anything?

BEAU. No. But I miss you.

FAN. I am here, aren't I? Some of us can do more than one
thing at once.

BEAU. Then can we do Christmas as well? Father and I are so
grateful for all your work, but –

FAN. Have either of you looked at these ledgers in recent
memory?

BEAU. We shall make it our first task in January, gladly –

FAN. Then you don't know.

BEAU. What? Of the farthing owing here, the penny missing
there?

FAN. Fezziwig's is in trouble, Beau. We spend more than we
earn.

BEAU. But the warehouse is busy all the time, Father seems happy –

FAN. Who wouldn't be happy with the amount of wine he drinks!

BEAU. Fan. My father is not your father.

FAN. All fathers are men. That they have such power despite considerable weakness is what unites them.

BEAU. Mine is not about to go to prison, and soon, yours will be free! Come on, put down that pen.

FAN. You have never known what it is like to be poor. Making every penny count, not wasting a crumb of bread, eking out every shard of coal.

BEAU. Please, no more of this. You had lost your home. We asked you to keep our books, as a kindness.

FAN. A kindness? Is that what it was?

BEAU. What happened to that carefree girl I fell in love with a year ago?

FAN. You mistook her, sir. She was never carefree. She sought purpose.

BEAU. Forgive me, but the original vacancy, as advertised –

FAN. As advertised –

BEAU. Was to be by my side. To love and be loved. I even dared to dream –

FAN. That I would give this up to raise your children? You will not be able to afford children if we do not fix this company!

BEAU. We are but a small provincial draper, Fan, not the East India Trading Company, doing things as my father's father did, and his before him. The past is not a bad place, Fan. Do not fear tradition. Like Parliament, this feast of Nativity itself – we will endure!

FAN. My past is only full of suffering. Can you not see how I must only think of the future?

BEAU. I do now. And you see a different one to me.

FAN. We could still share it –

BEAU. Only on your terms, and I can't accept that. This is my house, and one day, my father's company will be mine.

FAN. And I your obedient wife and mother to your children.

BEAU. You speak as if I was forcing you into slavery, not offering up a life of married bliss!

FAN. I only knew one marriage in my short life so far, and it was as far from bliss as it is possible to be on earth. It is not my dream.

BEAU. Then I have you wrong, and it is you who must forgive me.

FAN *nods and stands up, gathering her things.*

You would leave me alone, on Christmas Eve?

FAN. I go as I came in. I am sure you will manage. You are not alone.

BEAU. I just want a relationship, not a revolution.

FAN. And I thought you were different, a mistake I will not make again.

BEAU. That makes two of us.

FAN. Will you remember me?

BEAU. As long as I shall live, Fan Scrooge.

SCROOGE *leaves the scene.* BEAU *is inconsolable.*

SCROOGE. Did he remember me, spirit?

PAST. Oh, look! You are shaking. Where did you go next?

SCROOGE. What else could I do? I lived amongst women, doing what piecework I could find, until I met a handsome young moneylender called Jacob Marley. I thought I loved him – but you must know all this, spirit! Answer my question! Please. Beau. Did he remember me?

PAST. We can only play in Christmases past, not today.

SCROOGE. Then show me what you can. I must know.

PAST. Very well. One last play! The most recent Christmas past I can show…

She waves her hand one more time, and BEAU'S SONS *run onto the stage, singing –*

Scene Seven

BEAU FEZZIWIG*'s residence, seven years ago. A Christmas tree, hung with candles and ribbons. His sons,* FRANK *and* SID, *laughing and carrying a* TURKEY ON A PLATTER, *are pursued by* CATHERINE, *their mother.*

SONS (*chants*). Little Jack Horner
    Sat in the corner,
    Eating a Christmas pie!

As they sing FRANK *passes the* TURKEY *over* CATHERINE*'s head to* SID.

He put in his thumb,
And pulled out a plum,
And said, 'Yum! Yum! Yum!
What a good boy am I!'

CATHERINE. Boys, I pray of you, stop this now, your father will be home soon, please give me back that bird –

And back, CATHERINE *chasing, and again, then as* FRANK *grabs it, they freeze, and the* TURKEY *speaks –*

TURKEY. The noise in the room was perfectly tumultuous as the young brigands pillaged the young woman. The consequences were uproarious beyond belief, but no one seemed to care – the mother laughed heartily and enjoyed it very much.

CATHERINE. Frank. Give me that blessed bird this instant, or there will be no Christmas and no presents!

FRANK. Like this one, Mother?

He picks up a present, and rips it open – a small pile of books.

I read them all already!

He chucks them over his shoulder.

SID (*producing a young baby, swaddled*). Look, Mother, I've got the baby! Shall we pass her like the turkey, too?

CATHERINE. For the love of God –

FRANK. Oh, Mother! I'm going to stick the turkey on top of the Christmas tree, and you can't stop me!

A fight over the bird, who briefly emerges from the scrum to declare –

TURKEY. Who would not have given anything to be that young woman then? The joy, and gratitude, and ecstasy! The immense relief as –

BEAU. I'm home!

The tree comes crashing down as BEAU *tumbles in, a flurry of scarves, a pile of presents toppling out of his arms.*

SONS. Father! Father! What have you got for us?

BEAU. All in good time, my little heroes! Now tell me, what mischief have you been up to? (*Sees devastation.*) What has been going on here?

SID. Mother knocked over the tree. We were helping her clear up.

FRANK. I tried to save the turkey, but...

BEAU. You young rascals! I bet you did! Now, off with you upstairs... and if you're extra good, I'm sure your mother will reward you with a bedtime story!

SONS. Yes, sir!

They race off.

BEAU (*embracing* CATHERINE). What. A. Day. I am exhausted. What's for dinner?

CATHERINE. I am sorry, it will be a little late this evening... the children have been... very high-spirited.

BEAU. Boys will be boys, my dear. No matter, I have plenty to attend to until we eat.

CATHERINE (*tidying up*). How goes everything at the warehouse?

BEAU. Let us just say that these trifles – (*Points to the presents.*) have me at the limit of our generosity. Business is hard. But we will weather the storm.

CATHERINE. We have no need to be alarmed, then.

BEAU. Absolutely none! Full steam ahead, and all that.

CATHERINE. You can always share any worries you have with me, you know.

BEAU. I would not want to worry that precious pretty head more than I need to.

CATHERINE. But I might be able to help –

BEAU. Now, you know what happened to the last woman who said that to me.

CATHERINE. I know. In fact... I saw her today.

BEAU. What, old busybody Scrooge?

CATHERINE. Or Mrs Marley, as she is now. Married to the moneylender in Cheap Street.

BEAU. How on earth do you know all this?

CATHERINE. I... went to see Mr Marley this morning.

BEAU. What on earth for?

CATHERINE. I worry, Beau. There is never enough money for everything you expect us to have –

BEAU. I told you, there is no need for any concern. Everything is under control. Fezziwig's has seen rougher seas and come through before.

CATHERINE. All the same, I thought – given all the expenses of the season – I should perhaps –

BEAU. I expressly forbid you to visit a moneylender again! We have no debts that we cannot meet... there are items that can be sold if needs be... what would people say?

CATHERINE. You have no need to be concerned. I was not even admitted. Jacob Marley lies at the point of death, his clerk told me. I caught a glimpse of Mrs Marley through the window. I do believe I never saw a woman as alone in the world as she.

BEAU. How desperate. What a waste of a life.

CATHERINE. Did you truly love her?

BEAU. I thought I did... but she made herself quite unlovable.

CATHERINE. There seemed to be a sadness deep within her.

BEAU. No wonder. Look at the life she could have had. The life *we* have.

CATHERINE. Indeed.

SCROOGE. No more! Spirit, I beg you. No more! Take me away, this instant.

PAST. Don't you like this game, Fan? I did not make the rules. Don't be cross with me, Fan.

SCROOGE. Why on earth should I be cross with you?

PAST. These people are so happy! I thought that might make you sad.

SCROOGE. How little you understand me, spirit. I am affected that my brief role in this man's life left him so little changed... if anything, I set him on a worse path.

PAST. All I want is for you to be happy, Fan.

SCROOGE. All this getting, this endless striving – for what?
It does not even make men happy.

PAST. Play with me. Play with us all. Open your heart, Fan
Scrooge, as you once did as a child. We all have more in
common than that which separates and divides us.

SCROOGE. I do not blame you, spirit, I blame Jacob Marley,
my wretched father, Beau Fezziwig, I blame the long
procession of men who made me who I am! Take me away
from them! Take me home!

PAST. And, look, it is as if we never left.

BEAU*'s home has disappeared.*

Is this what you truly want? A cold bed?

SCROOGE. Yes.

PAST. This dark and lonely bedroom.

SCROOGE. And how.

PAST. You still do not see, do you?

SCROOGE. I see that you have overstayed your welcome. Why
did Marley send you to torment me? Whatever my late
husband wants me to do, or be, I say, I never will. Tell him
that from me. Do you understand?

PAST. Another will come –

But SCROOGE *takes the extinguisher cap, and douses the
candle and the spirit.*

SCROOGE. Let them try!

Scene Eight

SCROOGE *is back in her bed, trying to sleep.*

The bell tolls again, as the clock strikes two.

SCROOGE (*waking*). Ha. Two. And all quiet. I see you got the message, Jacob.

A thud shakes the stage.

What is that?

Another. Then another, like giant's footsteps.

Do your worst, Jacob Marley! You gave me no peace on earth, and now you do the same from the grave!

Now there is a banging against the doors, and walls – something trying to get in.

Well, I am no more afeared of your phantoms, do you hear?

The doors rattle, the stage is thumped from below, the bell shakes, rings crazily.

I will not be manipulated, or bullied, not any more!

It feels like the theatre is about to take off or explode.

I am not afraid!

She hides under the covers, as this rises to a shattering crescendo of shaking frames, doors, windows, bells and chimes.

I am mistress of my own home. Mistress of my body and my mind. I will not be overcome!

The footsteps are deafening, the bed shudders, the bell shakes fit to fall on us all –

SCROOGE*'s dressing gown flies from the bedroom door, monstrously animated as if with a life of its own.*

And then, bursting out of it in Hulk-like fashion, a towering giant, with something of the ancient wood about him –

The GHOST OF CHRISTMAS PRESENT.

PRESENT. Look upon me!

SCROOGE. I cannot.

PRESENT. You have never seen the like of me before.

SCROOGE. No! And nor do I wish to! Leave me in peace, ghost.

PRESENT. LOOK UPON ME!

SCROOGE. Just now, one of your number showed me my past, moments and memories I was long since familiar with. I will not venture there again. What manner of creature are you?

PRESENT. I have come to connect you with an even better time. The only space I can live in. The present! Try and be a bit more 'now', Scrooge! Touch my robe, and see what it feels like to live in the moment.

SCROOGE. I struggle to think of anything I would like to do less.

PRESENT. Touch my robe!

SCROOGE. I'll just go back to bed, but thanks for the offer.

PRESENT. Touch my robe.

SCROOGE. Ask a third time and I shall lodge a complaint.

PRESENT. So be it!

He sweeps her up in his robe and they vanish magically into the darkness, PRESENT's *laughter echoing all around. In their place stand two* CHILDREN, *alone with their* CAT.

IGNORANCE. Are they doing that ghost thing again?

WANT. Looks like it. I just want to stop moving and rest.

IGNORANCE. Come on, sis. Not far now.

MEAGRE. They flew high above the city. The house fronts below were black, and the windows blacker still, contrasting with the smooth white snow upon the roofs. The sky was gloomy, and far down below the shorter streets were choked up with a dingy mist, the dirty snow on the ground ploughed up in deep furrows by the heavy wheels of carts and wagons, turned into thick yellow mud and icy water.

IGNORANCE. 'There's no place like home.'

WANT. There's no home for us. Ever. Please make it stop. Somebody!

PRESENT *reappears, bearing* SCROOGE *with him. They look out at the audience.*

SCROOGE. I have never seen the city from such a great height before. Why do you show me these people? Look at them all!

PRESENT. I'm really interested that you asked me that question. Why do *you* think I'm showing you?

SCROOGE. There's a lot of them. Where do they all come from? I don't recognise any of them. They neither owe me money and nor have they asked to borrow any – (*Peers more closely.*) Yet.

PRESENT. I used to be the same as you. Moody, self-absorbed. And then, do you know what I discovered?

SCROOGE. The sound of your own voice?

PRESENT. Meditation! An hour every day, create a clear space in your head, feel the universal flow of life. We are all connected!

SCROOGE. I feel perfectly alive without connecting to that lot down there, thanks. Look at the state! Some of them can't have washed for a week.

PRESENT. I'm sensing a lot of hostility here, Scrooge. Close your eyes, count to ten, and as you do, visualise the words 'Christmas is time for everyone to celebrate and share together.' (*To audience.*) Come on, everybody, after me:

'Christmas is time for everyone to celebrate and share together!'

He waits till he gets a response and plays with it.

SCROOGE. Not for me it isn't! They're welcome to it.

PRESENT. Then think of a time which does make you happy. Do not blame them.

SCROOGE. Do not blame me for their problems either. There are men, and women. Children. Individuals all. They must look to themselves first, and we must look after ourselves.

PRESENT. And when they cannot look after themselves?

SCROOGE. My door is always open, my rates very reasonable.

PRESENT. You're going to be like *that*, are you? Very well. Off we go!

PRESENT *sighs and picks her up again.*

They disappear once more, as the company create FREDERICA*'s home.*

Scene Nine

We hear the strains of 'The Ditchling Carol'…

The piano and carol grow louder.

SCROOGE. Wait, ghost, what is that sound?

PRESENT. You know this music?

SCROOGE. All too well.

FREDERICA*'s home. She is playing the piano (aided by* FROU-FROU) *while her husband's friend* TOPPER, *blindfolded, chases her husband* NEVILLE *in a game of Blind Man's Buff.*

It cannot be.

PRESENT. Try and be happy just for once! Smile! Look! Your niece has inherited your musical talents.

SCROOGE. Not just my talents.

PRESENT. I see… that is your piano too?

SCROOGE. It was. When I married Marley it became his, and when he died… he left it to her.

PRESENT. What a generous guy. To encourage her in her talent, I presume.

SCROOGE. No, to spite me.

TOPPER *fumbles and gropes* FREDERICA.

TOPPER. Aha! I've got you now! You have an unmistakeable rear, Neville!

He is neither groping NEVILLE *nor a rear.*

FREDERICA. Topper! (*Wriggles free*). You can stop now. Neville! Can you believe that this once used to belong to Aunt Fan?

NEVILLE. I find it hard to conceive of your aunt playing a game of cards, never mind a piano. She has hardened her heart against all pleasure.

TOPPER. Counting coins in her money house! Clink clink, eh! That's the only music she plays!

FREDERICA. I think you are too hard on poor Aunt Fan.

FROU-FROU (*to* FREDERICA). Go on, give us a biscuit.

FREDERICA *reluctantly does*.

TOPPER. Poor! That is not what I heard.

NEVILLE. They say she has half the wealth of the City of London stuffed under her mattress. She would be a fine match for… you, my dear Topper!

TOPPER. I may be alone but I am not desperate!

NEVILLE (*high-pitched impression of Scrooge*). Ooh but I like a bit of meat on a man… to get my claws into!

TOPPER (*matching his take*). Ooh, don't mind if I do –

FREDERICA. Stop it! You are both too unkind.

SCROOGE. The girl has a voice. Well, I never.

FREDERICA. I went to see her this morning, in fact. I invited her to Christmas.

FROU-FROU. More guests. More PRESENTS!

SCROOGE. You see, she will vouch for me!

NEVILLE. Oh no. You didn't, did you? Why on earth?

FREDERICA. If you must know... I felt sorry for her.

FROU-FROU. I was sad too. Look at my sad face. I'm weeping on the inside.

The watching SCROOGE *tries to wriggle away from* PRESENT –

SCROOGE. Take me away from this place, spirit! Take me away right now.

PRESENT. Progress! An honest feeling at last.

SCROOGE. Far from it. She's started pitying me, and really I would rather stick needles in my eyeballs than watch another second.

But he makes her do just that.

FREDERICA. Don't worry. She said no. She said that Christmas was – a humbug!

TOPPER. This? A humbug? She is misery incarnate, I tell you!

FREDERICA. But who does she injure with her misery? Not you, Topper, or even me. Only herself! Now she must dine all alone on Christmas Day.

SCROOGE *is desperate, trying to reach into the scene –*

SCROOGE. Ghost – let me talk to her!

PRESENT. Would that I could. This is but a living dream.

SCROOGE. They are wrong. They misunderstand me entirely.

PRESENT. Or do you misunderstand them?

SCROOGE. I understand them perfectly well. It has been the tragedy of my life to be misunderstood. A crime I did not commit, and yet will never be forgiven for.

NEVILLE *slaps the piano.*

NEVILLE. Then that is her loss, and her choice! So let us put Aunt Fan out of our minds, dear wife, and enjoy what she never will. Play it again!

FROU-FROU. Calling Miss Frederica to the stage! Encore, maestro!

FREDERICA. Very well. And Merry Christmas and a Happy New Year to the old girl, wherever she is!

FREDERICA *begins to play 'The Ditchling Carol' again – and the bright and jolly gathering disappears into the night as it came.*

Scene Ten

MEAGRE. Invisibly, the spirit swept Scrooge on to the outskirts of the city, where they now stood below a very low roof, of an altogether more modest and humble dwelling.

SCROOGE. The middle of nowhere! Who on earth would live here?

MRS CRATCHIT *appears as the carol picks up pace.*

Humming along to the tune, she 'makes' a complete Christmas feast, from laying the place settings to preparing the food and trimmings.

However it is achieved, the result should be the suggestion of a miniature banqueting scene of the finest quality, seemingly out of nothing other than the most tireless industry of one woman and magical enough to elicit a round of applause, even from SCROOGE.

BOB CRATCHIT *returns with* TINY TIM, *who is wheezing.*
They wrap him in a blanket.

CRATCHIT. Well, I don't know about you, but I am *exhausted.*
Where's our dinner?

MRS CRATCHIT. Bless your heart alive, my dear, how late
you are!

CRATCHIT. The church service didn't half go on – I thought at
one point we might be still there next Christmas.

MRS CRATCHIT. And how did Tiny Tim behave?

CRATCHIT. As good as gold –

TINY TIM. I can speak for myself, Father. I may not be able to
breathe as others can, but I can think and speak as good as
any my age.

MRS CRATCHIT. And many older who should be wiser. Tell us
then, Tim.

TINY TIM. We were sat at the back –

CRATCHIT. That we were.

TINY TIM. Only I asked Father to find us space at the front.

CRATCHIT. Which I did, after much excusing and shoving and
squeezing.

TINY TIM. For I wanted 'em all to see me. On this morning.
Being afflicted as I am.

MRS CRATCHIT. What on earth for, my love?

TINY TIM. So that they should remember.

MRS CRATCHIT. Remember what?

TINY TIM. That today is Christmas Day, Mother! A day of
miracles! Jesus cured the incurable. And one day I hope he
should do the same for me.

MRS CRATCHIT. Oh, we all hope that.

CRATCHIT. We do indeed. And on that note – a Merry
Christmas to us all, my dears! God bless us all!

TINY TIM. God bless us, every one.

CRATCHIT *rises to his feet with a glass, to make a toast.*

CRATCHIT. May I raise a glass to she, whom without, we would have nothing?

MRS CRATCHIT. The Queen?

CRATCHIT. Only in my world of work, my dear – Miss Scrooge.

MRS CRATCHIT. Raise a glass to her? If ever she shows her face around here, I'll raise more than a glass to 'er!

CRATCHIT. Dear wife! *Tiny Tim!*

MRS CRATCHIT. But you said you gave her a book… revolution is coming, you said!

CRATCHIT. Perhaps I did. But now I have had a glass of this excellent wine, and dear wife – it is Christmas Day.

MRS CRATCHIT. Very well. Because I am a Christian – and *only* because I am a Christian, mind – to Miss Scrooge!

Their glasses clink!

SCROOGE (*aside*). Look how she gives in so readily. I had hoped for more from Mrs Cratchit. I had hoped that of all women, she might share my resolve. Well. The more fool them. I do not require it. I do not toast them!

MRS CRATCHIT. Now, Tim, will you sing for us, as you always do?

With considerable but dignified effort, TINY TIM *solemnly stands on a chair, with a glass. He sings the poem, 'A Child's Hymn' by Charles Dickens.*

TINY TIM. Hear my prayer, O heavenly Father,
Ere I lay me down to sleep;
Bid Thy angels, pure and holy,
Round my bed their vigil keep.
Keep me through this night of peril
Underneath its boundless shade;

Take me to Thy rest, I pray Thee,
When my pilgrimage is made.
Pardon all my past transgressions,
Give me strength for days to come;
Guide and guard me with Thy blessing
Till Thy angels bid me home.

Silence.

SCROOGE. Ghost, tell me something. Does their child live?

PRESENT. I don't wish to be negative but… I fear a vacant seat
by this happy table in years to come. A blanket without an
owner, carefully preserved. If these shadows remain
unaltered, the child will perish.

SCROOGE. Then that is a great pity.

PRESENT. Can you unpack that statement for me?

SCROOGE. Let him be put to some good use before his time on
earth expires! His father has often complained to me about
his workload – I would gladly let his son take on his more
menial duties.

PRESENT. How very generous of you.

SCROOGE. Naturally, given his lack of qualifications, this
would be unwaged. But it's good experience.

PRESENT. For what? The grave?

SCROOGE. Do not paint me the villain, spirit! I did not make
this world of work! I only seek to survive in it.

PRESENT. No, you merely seek to profit from it! Now, quiet –
for there is more to see!

*He sweeps away the Cratchit Christmas with a flourish of his
robe, and as the clock strikes a quarter to three, a lonely,
moaning wind surrounds them.*

Scene Eleven

A dark, cold and miserable place, winds howling all around.

SCROOGE. What happened, ghost, where did they go?

PRESENT. The problem with living in the moment is that my life is very short. It ends tonight at three. Our time together is nearly up, friend.

SCROOGE. What is this frightful place? Where have you brought me now?

PRESENT. Nowhere.

SCROOGE. It must be somewhere.

PRESENT. Nowhere you have heard of. Nowhere to anybody but those for whom it is their only place of refuge.

SCROOGE. But there is no one here.

PRESENT. Aha! No one that you have noticed. Focus, and look again.

A hand appears through his ghostly robes, seemingly out of nowhere.

SCROOGE. What is this claw?

PRESENT. It might be a claw, for all the flesh that remains upon it. Go on, take it.

SCROOGE. If this is some trick –

PRESENT. I wish it were.

SCROOGE *takes the hand and pulls out, as if from a void,* IGNORANCE, *grabbing* WANT, *who clutches* MEAGRE. *They collapse at her feet, a wasted pile. The wind grows fiercer still.*

SCROOGE. They are – that is – are they yours, ghost?

PRESENT. They are humankind's.

SCROOGE. It's quite impossible, but even so – I feel that I have seen them before.

IGNORANCE. We was in the street when you walked by.

WANT. At yer winder, yer door.

MEAGRE. They were a boy and a girl. Where graceful youth should have filled their features out, and touched them with its freshest tints, a stale and shrivelled hand, like age, had pinched, and twisted them and pulled them into shreds.

IGNORANCE *and* WANT. And you never even noticed!

PRESENT. You have seen them everywhere. This boy is Ignorance, the girl Want. Do you deny that you have seen them?

WANT *collapses,* IGNORANCE *clutches her. The* GHOST *fades as the clock tolls three.*

And that's all we have time for, folks. I'm outta here.

SCROOGE. Don't leave me here! Not alone with these children! They need help... food... medicine... warmth! Where can I take them?

PRESENT. 'Are there no prisons? Are there no workhouses?'

SCROOGE. Ghost! I cannot help these wretches!

PRESENT (*as he leaves*). Well... perhaps if you had borne some of your own you would know how.

SCROOGE (*grabs his sleeve*). Wait! What did you say?

PRESENT. If you had borne your own –

SCROOGE. *If I had borne my own?* No. You have no idea of what I have borne, or tried to, what I have suffered. What I have endured. What I have wished for or not. Do not lay that at my feet, ghost.

PRESENT. Another will come. Open your heart before it is too late.

SCROOGE. I did open my heart, a long time ago, and look where it got me!

PRESENT. Your heart is closed up to the world. Admit it!

SCROOGE. I admit only that I am a woman and I have lived the life that men made for me. Well, no more, ghost. Do you hear me? And your fellow phantoms, and my dead husband too? I will not apologise. I will not explain. I did little out of choice. Send me an army of phantom men to haunt my every moment's sleep! I will not repent!

The storm reaches its wintry, thundery climax… and WANT *faints in* SCROOGE's *arms, who sinks to the ground, holding the* CHILDREN *tight to her as the heavens open above their heads.*

I will not!

End of Act One.

ACT TWO

Scene One

As the audience return to their seats, IGNORANCE *and* WANT *move through them as before, enquiring after their interval, before beginning again on a bare stage.*

A mist spreads.

IGNORANCE. So, like, are we dead now?

WANT. We would be if those kind people hadn't given us some of their water, and their ice cream.

IGNORANCE. That was amazing wasn't it? (*Looks out into the audience and sighs.*) I didn't know they had ice creams in heaven.

WANT. Oh, brother! I don't think we are in heaven after all.

IGNORANCE. You can say that again! Look at this place. It could do with a lick of paint, couldn't it? Then... where are we?

WANT. Who can say? I only know that I still want to live! I want to keep on living and striving, despite it all.

IGNORANCE. Me too. I thought we were goners there for a moment. Still, at least we know who we are now, eh? I'm... wait, what was I called again?

WANT. I wish I could remember. I just want someone to say what happens to us.

IGNORANCE. I know. If only I'd heard this story before I might have a clue, but...

He shrugs.

WANT. Does it ever end?

IGNORANCE. I'll be having words with that bloody cat if it doesn't.

WANT. But even at the end, we never truly die, do we?

IGNORANCE. And we never truly live.

The company begin to sing, softly, 'The Ditchling Carol', in a haunting arrangement.

COMPANY (*sings*). Be merry all, be merry all
With holly dress the festive hall,
Prepare the song, the feast, the hall…

Singing continues under the next exchange.

WANT. We are always here, whether you like it or not.

IGNORANCE. Whether we like it or not!

WANT. All we want is to be down there!

IGNORANCE. With you. Wrapped up warm with families and friends.

WANT. Going home at the end.

IGNORANCE. Knowing that next day might be different… or better.

WANT. All we want is for our story to be more like yours.

IGNORANCE. If only we knew someone who could help with that…

They fade away, MEAGRE *taking their place, and we are back with* SCROOGE *in her bedroom, as we were before.*

SCROOGE *sits bolt upright in bed as if waking from a nightmare.*

SCROOGE. No! I will not! Wait – where am I? What day is it now, can anyone tell me? It is so cold. Why do I shiver?

COMPANY. Be merry all, be merry all
With holly dress the festive hall,
Prepare the song, the feast, the hall!

Then there is something in, underneath, on the bed beside her – her own sheets, twisting in horrific form –

MEAGRE. A phantom silently approached. In the very air in which this spirit moved it seemed to scatter gloom and mystery.

SCROOGE. Another? I can't believe this. Which spectre are you now?

COMPANY. Be merry all, be merry all
With holly dress the festive hall,
Prepare the song, the feast, the hall!

The twisted and stretched bedsheets take a spectral form.

SCROOGE. What do you want?

The sheet spirit extends a silent ghostly, draped hand, pointing at her.

From me? What? I have nothing for you. Tell me your name, phantom!

MEAGRE. The mysterious presence filled her with a solemn dread. The spirit answered not, but pointed onwards with what stood for its hand.

IGNORANCE (*appearing*). Ooh. I don't like the look of that one. Are we dead now?

WANT. Might as well be – as far as she's concerned. I want to live, brother! I want to keep on living, despite it all.

SCROOGE. Follow my own bedsheets? Are you mad? Tell me your name, curse you!

COMPANY. Be merry all, be merry all
With holly dress the festive hall,
Prepare the song, the feast, the hall!

SCROOGE. I was warned to expect three. Are you the Ghost of Christmas Yet to Come? I fear you more than any spirit I have seen… and yet I doubt even you can move me. Will you not speak?

The GHOST OF CHRISTMAS FUTURE *is impassive and unmoved.* SCROOGE *is surrounded by the* COMPANY, *who lift her up and carry her out after* FUTURE, *as the music rises to a crescendo.*

Very well! Then show me what you must!

COMPANY. Be merry all, be merry all
With holly dress the festive hall,
Prepare the song, the feast, the ball!

Scene Two

MEAGRE. Then the ghost drew Scrooge on to an obscure and dark part of town.

A match flares in the darkness to light a lamp, but the scene stays dark.

A rattle of metal. SCROOGE *and* FUTURE *appear.*

The ways were foul and narrow, the shops and houses wretched, the people drunken and ugly, the whole quarter reeking with filth, crime and misery – there stood a low-browed shop of infamous repute, where iron, old rags, bottles and even bones were bought by their owners, in search of a penny or two in exchange.

Two people, barely visible, partly obscured by piles of junk and rags.

MRS DILBER. What you got from her, then?

JOE. What ain't I got? What odds, Mrs Dilber, what odds!

MRS DILBER. Don't you mind it, Joe. Every person has a right to look after themselves. She always did, and no mistake.

SCROOGE. A sensible woman. I like her immediately. Who are they talking about, ghost?

JOE. Very well then! She won't miss these where she's going!

He unfurls a bundle... SCROOGE*'s bed curtains.*

MRS DILBER. Ooh, Joe, now these are fine! How do you get these?

SCROOGE. They look just like *my* bed curtains.

JOE. I took 'em down, didn't I?

MRS DILBER. But how'd you get in – not while she was still lying there! You never!

JOE. She's not going to mind now, is she? I saw her lying naked there, and trust me, she isn't going to get any colder.

MRS DILBER. Ha! It's too bad, isn't it. In life, she frightened everyone away from her. Now, in death, she can't even hold on to her own curtains. And we, you and I, are to profit from it.

JOE. Is that worse than how she profited from men and women while alive?

MRS DILBER. I can't say it is!

SCROOGE. Very good, spirit. I see you mean to teach me a moral lesson, by example. This poor unfortunate woman whose house they have plundered, you suggest the same fate awaits me? You mean to cower me by showing me these criminals? Nice try. I care not what happens after my death. I live my life according to my own rules.

FUTURE *points again to the scene.*

MRS DILBER. Now. Let us cut to the chase, Joe. Curtains and what-have-you are very fine, very fine indeed, but were there, without being indelicate, any items of interest on her person?

JOE. There might have been, Mrs Dilber!

MRS DILBER. Go on then!

JOE. I'm not sure I should... it was very intimate.

MRS DILBER (*grabs him*). Show me what you got, old man,
    unless you wants to join her in the earth?

JOE. But will you pay the price?

He produces a gold ring from his pocket.

SCROOGE. My goodness. That looks just like the ring Beau
    once gave me!

MRS DILBER. What a beauty. Unlike its owner.

SCROOGE. You scoundrels! Stealing jewellery from a corpse.
    Why do you show me these rogues, phantom? I am a
    moneylender, not a mere pawnbroker. How do you mean to
    shame me here?

JOE. Isn't it just. Look at it sparkle, Mrs Dilber.

MRS DILBER (*biting it*). But a fraud, Joe, a fraud, just like her.
    Next!

SCROOGE. Well it cannot have been my ring, then. Beau
    would never have given me something so worthless.

   MRS DILBER *tosses it onto a heap of costume jewellery
   next to her. She and* JOE *laugh heartily.*

   Are their hearts so hardened? It does not surprise me, but is
   there no one in this great city who feels something at the
   passing of this poor woman?

   *The laughter continues, growing and amplified, echoing
   around* SCROOGE's *ears with the sound of clinking coins as*
   FUTURE *sweeps her on –*

Scene Three

WANT. Then that ghost spread her sheets one more time, and there was a plain old room in a rough part of town.

IGNORANCE. A girl waits for her father.

A girl, AMY DORSET, *comes in with her sewing.*

WANT. Do you remember our father, brother? Do you think he'll ever come back for us?

IGNORANCE. Don't be daft.

WANT. I want to see him again. Just one last time.

IGNORANCE. Like all of Scrooge's customers, the father owed her loads of money.

WANT. They're nearly as poor as us!

IGNORANCE. Then they should sell each other. (*To* WANT.) I'd sell you if I had to.

WANT. You would and all. (*Beat.*) Would yer really?

IGNORANCE. Never. Not even to save me own life. Never.

WANT. We're in this together to the end, aren't we, brother?

IGNORANCE. The bitter end.

SCROOGE. She looks sensible, of a fair and tender heart. I do not recognise her, but perhaps she is making something to remember this poor woman by. Is that it, ghost?

AMY*'s father,* WILLIAM DORSET, *rushes in.*

Ah! I know him. William Dorset, a very regular customer. But a bad payer. You remind me, when I wake up, I must send word to Cratchit to collect what is owing –

AMY. Tell me straight, Father, is it good or bad?

WILLIAM. Bad.

AMY. Then we are ruined.

WILLIAM. No, there is hope yet, sweetest Amy.

AMY. Only if she relents!

WILLIAM. She is past relenting. She is dead.

AMY. Oh… to whom will our debt be transferred? Will you be spared prison, Father? Please tell me.

WILLIAM. I don't know, but perhaps it will give us more time to find the money we need?

AMY. I am sewing as fast as I can, Father.

WILLIAM. Worry not, sweet child. I know you are. Even if you cannot, it would be bad luck indeed to find a successor as our creditor who was as heartless and cold as she. We will sleep with light hearts tonight!

SCROOGE. That death gives them pleasure, does it not? A kind of liberty. Then perhaps it has not been in vain. They will still pay their debts. I wonder who they speak of. (*Aside*.) It cannot be of me.

FUTURE *stares at her.*

It cannot be of me.

A humming begins, the tune of the song below, as FUTURE *sweeps her on.*

Scene Four

As MEAGRE *narrates over the humming, so we move on.*

MEAGRE. The ghost conducted Scrooge through several
    streets which seemed familiar to her – although she saw no
    sign of herself in them – until they reached an iron gate, and
    beyond it – a churchyard!

    CRATCHIT *and* MRS CRATCHIT *emerge, in their Sunday
    best, singing a version of 'A Child's Hymn', led by the*
    PRIEST.

SCROOGE. They must be going to church, on Christmas
    morning! But… where is the little one?

PRIEST. Let us pray!

MRS CRATCHIT (*sings*). Hear my prayer, O heavenly Father,
    Ere I lay me down to sleep;
    Bid Thy angels, pure and holy,
    Round my bed their vigil keep.

MEAGRE. They all walked a little slower of late. Even though
    with Tiny Tim upon his shoulders, Bob Cratchit had been
    known to walk very fast indeed.

CRATCHIT (*sings*). My sins are heavy, but Thy mercy
    Far outweighs them, every one;
    Down before Thy cross I cast them,
    Trusting in Thy help alone.

MEAGRE. You see, he was so light to carry. And they loved
    him so, that he was no trouble at all. No trouble at all.

SCROOGE. But where is he? Where is the little one?

MEAGRE. It was a green place, and they had promised each
    other they would always walk there on a Sunday.

IGNORANCE. Hang on, I think I know this place.

SCROOGE. Where? Where are they going?

CRATCHITS (*singing together*). Pardon all my past
transgressions,
Give me strength for days to come;
Guide and guard me with Thy blessing
Till Thy angels bid me home.

The PRIEST *summons a small gravestone out of the ground,
covered in snow, and bows his head.*

SCROOGE. Do not show me this, spirit! Do not show me!

WELL-WISHER 1 (*off*). I am heartily sorry for it, Mr Cratchit!

WELL-WISHER 2 (*off*). And I am sorry for your good wife!

FREDERICA (*off*). Oh, Mr Cratchit! If ever there is anything
I can do, then please, let me know!

SCROOGE. My niece! But what did *I* say to them? Please tell
me I had a kind word.

The family pay their respects at TINY TIM*'s grave in silence
for a moment, and then* CRATCHIT *collapses.*

PRIEST. We are gathered here, to remember –

CRATCHIT (*weeping*). My little, little child! My little child!
(*To* MRS CRATCHIT.) Promise me you will never forget
him, Ann!

MRS CRATCHIT. I promise!

CRATCHIT. And promise me that if we ever quarrel amongst
ourselves, we shall remember how mild he was, and kind.

CRATCHITS. Forever.

SCROOGE. Ghost, the first of your kind intimated that it might
be possible to speak with one of these phantoms, if I so
desired… I implore you, take me to my future self, so that
I may entreat her to have a kind word.

FUTURE *points back to the gravestone, as the* CRATCHITS
and the PRIEST *depart.*

I don't understand –

Another gravestone rises beyond TINY TIM*'s.*

Before I draw nearer to that stone, tell me, spirit – are these the shadows of things that will be, or that may be?

FUTURE *points to the grave.*

MEAGRE. This second stone was in a wretched corner of the churchyard, overrun by grass and weeds.

IGNORANCE. I knew it! Where we buried that old bloke! Except this is in an even worse part. Gives me the shivers it does.

MEAGRE. Scrooge read upon the neglected stone her own name. Fan Scrooge.

SCROOGE. Am I the woman whose bed those thieves robbed?

FUTURE *nods.*

Am I the woman whose death the Dorsets cheered?

It nods again.

Am I the woman whose death no one mourned? No!

SCROOGE *sinks to the ground, in front of the grave.*

I am not that woman!

Then, slowly, deliberately, she confronts FUTURE *in fury.*

Why show me this if I am past all hope? Why show me my grave? Why show me the death of a child? This is Jacob Marley's doing. You are trying to manipulate me, and it will not work, do you hear? I am simply trying to earn a living. Or would you rather I joined Tiny Tim in his pauper's grave over there? You have shown me a night of shadows, all of you, and they have confirmed in me one thing. I was born into a world of fathers, of owners, of rule-makers. I seek only to balance the ledger, for that is what I am trained to do. Let women have their account, and be responsible for it. Tell my former husband that he can raise demons from the depths of hell, send every floating spectre from the heavenly realm to shame me, lecture me, control me, but it will never work!

Not for this Christmas or the one after that. (*Aside*.) For I am
no worse than he! I am not this woman, but let it be known
to the living and the dead, that I *am* a woman! And I will
never change!

*She grabs at the ghost, which crumples and falls limp in her
hands.*

COMPANY (*singing softly*). And when in scenes of glory
We sing the new, new song
'Twill be the old, old story
That we have loved so long!
'Twill be the old, old story
That we have loved so long!

IGNORANCE. Was that meant to happen?

MEAGRE. No, it was not! This is most irregular. This is not
how it goes.

IGNORANCE. So now what?

MEAGRE. Give me a moment! I need to think, perhaps go for
a walk –

IGNORANCE. A walk! We haven't got time!

*And with a WRENCHING, CRASHING sound, everything
Victorian is removed, including them, until we are left with –*

Scene Five

Working lights on a bare stage. The emptiness of Purgatory.
A low mist over the void.

MARLEY *appears, vexed, dragging his chains, surrounded by*
the three GHOSTS – PAST, PRESENT a*nd* FUTURE.

MARLEY. What do you mean it hasn't worked? Do you know
how much effort it was to send three ghosts back to haunt
my widow? It doesn't just happen, you know! You're all
lucky I was buried with some gold coins in my pockets. The
worst money I ever spent, dead or alive, as it happens. I want
a refund.

FUTURE *shrugs*.

(*To the others*.) Can it truly not speak, or was that just for
effect?

PAST. It's a bedsheet, what do you think?

MARLEY. Either give me my money back, or do what I asked!
Change Scrooge!

PRESENT. I was so close! Why don't I take her on a silent
retreat?

FUTURE *gives a massive double thumbs-up*.

MARLEY. A *silent* retreat? Have you met my wife?

PAST. There are lots of other Christmases past we didn't play
in. I showed her 1805, 1806, 1812, 1838. We could look at
1824, also 1825, 1826, 1827, 1828 –

MARLEY. Yes, thank you, I get the idea. What about your
friend in the sheet? Any bright ideas?

FUTURE *mimes something horrific*.

PRESENT. You never know where to draw the line, do you?

PAST. She's a phantom of the future, give her a break.

MARLEY. Oh, it's a she, is it? Well, that explains a great deal.
Never get a female ghost to do a man's job.

FUTURE *tries to choke him.*

Fine, fine, have it your way! But we need a new plan. I don't want to stay in this limbo forever, with these wretched chains! They're kind of dragging me down.

FUTURE *cringes at the joke.*

PAST. Perhaps you should have thought of that before you were so mean to everybody. Including your wife.

MARLEY. I can't change the past! I thought if I could get her to change, she could atone for both of us. It would cancel out my own sins as well. I wanted her to get rid of my chains!

FUTURE *has a laughing fit.*

PRESENT. I'm afraid it doesn't really work like that… listen, Jacob, I'm a great believer in acceptance. Here's what we're going to do. I'm going to make you the most beautiful turmeric latte and then we're going to find a mountaintop somewhere, watch the sunset together, and chant –

MARLEY. You are lucky you're a ghost, because that means I can't actually kill you.

PAST. Scrooge is haunted by her past… but also a product of it. We have reminded her of the person she once was, shown her the damage she does to those around her, and warned of where such a path will lead and yet…

PRESENT. She's not for turning. For all her faults, I do admire her commitment to being a miserable miser.

MARLEY. Please help me! I know I was a bad person! But I will do anything to get rid of these chains!

PRESENT. Well, if she does change, thanks to us, neither you or she will be bound by the chains you now wear. *If* she does.

MARLEY. Bloody women. She never could do what she was told. It was meant to be so simple. A fairy tale!

PAST. Some argue that fairy tales only exist to perpetuate the patriarchy.

MARLEY. Don't try and muddle me with long words! Just tell me what you're going to do.

FUTURE *whispers in* PAST*'s ear.*

I thought you said it couldn't talk!

PAST. Do you speak bedsheet?

MARLEY. Not really.

PAST. Well, then. There is one more possibility. Perhaps she has closed her heart to Christmas, to charity, to kindness, even to love, because she believes that as a woman it is the only way for her to survive her age. But what if we showed her –

PRESENT. A sunbeam illuminating the rainbow of eternity?

PAST. No! What if we showed her that there might be another time to be a woman?

MARLEY. You mean what will come of all this talk of the rights of women?

PRESENT. Oh, very good. Wish I'd thought of that. I try to live in the moment, all the time, that's my problem.

MARLEY. Just how far into the future can your silent friend take her?

PAST. There's only one way to find out…

FUTURE *disappears her colleagues and* MARLEY *with a wave of her hand, as we hear a clock going backwards at great speed, and we find ourselves back –*

Scene Six

The graveyard. SCROOGE *is still there, just as we left her.*

FUTURE *approaches.*

SCROOGE. I thought I'd made myself quite clear. Leave me in peace to mourn my wasted life.

FUTURE *shakes its head and points again.*

No, ghost. I do not want to see any more Christmases, past, present or future. My mind is made up. Why can you, and that dead wretch Marley, not understand – Christmas is not my time. Its memory brings me only pain and sorrow. I have closed my heart to survive this world I find myself in, and nothing you can show me will persuade me to open it again –

FUTURE *starts to drag* SCROOGE *away, as she screams and protests, we hear the clock again, now moving forward.*

Time-travel through sound, from church bells and horses to motor cars, telephones, aeroplanes, computers, phone notifications, the sounds of a modern urban Christmas…

Bars of glowing light create a modern space.

(*To* FUTURE.) What is this? Where are you taking me!

MEAGRE (*playing catch-up*). The phantom leads Scrooge on as it had before, swept up in her shadow, as they return from the green hill of the graveyard to the city. Only it is not… a city Scrooge… or I recognise. But all the same, there they are, right in the heart of it – glass towers glittering with electric light, the streets full of motorised vehicles and… shoppers lost in the gaze of little blue screens. And at the top of one such glass tower, in an office of glass walls, in the same city, it appears to be the eve of the same festival of Christmas, but… a hundred and seventy-four years later!

IGNORANCE (*to* MEAGRE). Surely it can't be worse than London in 1845? Can it?

FIONA SCROOGE *peers at the glow of a laptop over her glasses, which keeps whooshing with email and other notifications.*

IGNORANCE. She looks familiar.

MEAGRE. Frederica Scrooge's great-great-great-granddaughter, Fiona Scrooge. A director of the payday lending firm MarleyScrooge.com, established by her ex-husband Jake Marley.

IGNORANCE. Is she any nicer than her great-great-great-whatsit?

A photo of her late husband and business partner JAKE MARLEY *stands next to the monitor, along with an* ALEXA.

FIONA. Alexa, what is the office temperature?

ALEXA. The office temperature is eighteen degrees.

FIONA. For God's sake. No wonder I'm freezing. Alexa, turn up the temperature.

ALEXA. Temperature is set by user Jacob Marley. I cannot override this.

FIONA. Jacob? He left the company months ago. Turn it up or I will turn you off!

ALEXA. Would you like me to play 'Turn It Up' by Peter Andre?

FIONA. I would like you to explain how my ex-husband can control access to the office air-conditioning as well as my children, when he was the one who left me!

ALEXA. Now playing 'Turn It Up' by Peter Andre.

The song begins.

You have a Skype call, from Freddie Scrooge. Would you like to accept this call?

FIONA. Freddie? For the love of God, no. Not now – these accounts are well over deadline as it is.

ALEXA. Accepting call.

FREDDIE SCROOGE, *her twenty-something nephew, in skiing gear, snow behind him, appears, as if on Skype, etc.*

FREDDIE. Hiiii, Auntie Fi!

FIONA. Hi, Freddie. Look, it's not a great time, we're really up against it with deadlines –

FREDDIE. Hi, Fi! Look, I'm calling from Mum's chalet in the Alps! We're having such a wicked time. Are you sure you don't want to come and join us?

FIONA. Quite sure... send your mum my love... but some of us have work to do.

FREDDIE. Come on, it's Christmas! Even Donald Trump is enjoying the snow.

FIONA. Donald Trump?

FREDDIE (*holding up* FROU-FROU). My new dog! Early Christmas present from Zara. Isn't the name absolutely hilaire?

FROU-FROU. Hilaire.

FREDDIE. Look, just turn your computer off and get on that plane and come and join us. We haven't seen you for so long.

FIONA. It's not that simple –

FREDDIE. Come on, Fi. You look knackered. Have you lost weight?

A knock at the door –

FIONA. Hang on, Freddie – Now what!

    BILL BULLABY, *a colleague, comes in, dressed up as Father Christmas, waving a charity bucket.*

    Hi, Bill, sorry, I'm actually on –

BILL (*full Santa mode*). Ho ho, little girl! Have you been a good girl this Christmas?

FIONA. Not a great time, Bill. What is it this year?

BILL. Would you like to sit on my knee and I'll tell you!

FIONA. Oh do piss off.

BILL (*removing beard*). Temper temper! I only wanted to see if you wanted to take part in our New Year fun run.

FIONA. Can't I just give some money?

BILL (*rattling bucket*). Indeed you can if you have any change –

FIONA. Do you take contactless?

BILL. Not yet. Come on the fun run. Please. It's the Company Social Responsibility policy, and no one wants to do it.

FIONA. I don't even know what it's for!

BILL. Does it matter? Cancer? Donkeys? Orphans? Something like that. Please, just sign up and I'll leave you be.

FIONA. Where is the run?

BILL. We're running the entire length of the M25. First weekend in January. You can come dressed as any animal you like.

FIONA. GET OUT.

ALEXA. Phone call from… Francesca Scrooge.

FREDDIE (*Skype*). Hello? Are you still there, Fi? What's going on?

ALEXA. Call accepted.

FRANCESCA SCROOGE, FIONA*'s eight-year-old daughter, is on the line.*

FRANCESCA (*speakers*). Mum!

FIONA. Hi, darling, I can't really talk now… did you get home from school okay? Did Agnetha pick you up… tell her there's some cold shepherd's pie in the fridge, she can bung it in the microwave…

FRANCESCA. Mum, you missed my Nativity play! I was playing Jesus!

BILL. She's playing Jesus? Cross-gender casting? Very 2019.

FIONA (*to* BILL). What are you still doing here? (*To phone*.) I didn't, did I? Why does no one put these things in my diary? Alexa! What are my engagements for today?

ALEXA. You have a spin class with Marco at six o'clock at Super Gym. You have a conference call with New York office, Laura and Jason, during spin class at six thirty. You have a breakfast meeting with –

FIONA. I've done all that! Now! Now! What are my engagements for now?

FRANCESCA. Mum! Are you listening?

FREDDIE. Is that you, Franmeister??

FRANCESCA. Fredster! Are you skiing?

FREDDIE. Yes, mate, it's lush, tell your mum to bring you!

FRANCESCA. Mum! I want to go skiing!

ALEXA. Francesca Nativity play, St John's Primary –

FIONA. Then why the hell didn't you alert me!

ALEXA. I do not respond well to bad language.

A high-pitched 'notification' alert.

This is your daily breast-pump reminder! Now pump!

FIONA *drops down to the filing cabinet and pulls it open, pulling out a large breast pump and a bottle.*

FIONA. Oh God! One minute, darling…

She starts to discreetly fill the bottle up.

BILL *picks up his phone, snaps a pic and starts typing – his tweet is somehow represented…*

BILL. So proud to have a modern boss who doesn't leave the office to breastpump #21stcenturywoman #teamscrooge.

FIONA. What the hell do you think you are doing? Can I not have one moment's privacy?

BILL. I'm putting it on our Instagram. Sends such a positive signal.

FIONA. For who?

FREDDIE. Fi! Come on! Come over! Drop everything!

FRANCESCA. Mum! Come home! Agnetha doesn't know how to put *Peppa Pig* on for the baby!

ALEXA. You have not walked enough steps today to reach your target. I recommend running on the spot for five minutes. Four fifty-nine… (*Counts down.*)

   FIONA *starts jogging, still pumping.*

   You have… eighteen… Christmas gifts on your list still to be bought, shall I order them now?

BILL. Come on, just sign up! Do something for other people for once, Fiona!

ALEXA. Jamie Oliver says no stress, put the bird in the oven now for a hassle-free Christmas filled with magical memories.

FREDDIE. Fi! We're fam! Come and see us! Come on holiday!

FIONA. Alexa! End call!

ALEXA. Would you like me to set a reminder for you to record *Doctor Who*?

FIONA. No! I hate time-travel!

FRANCESCA. You're the worst mother in the world! I hate you! I don't even want you to come home for Christmas.

   The Peter Andre, calls, notifications, timer and all rise to a cacophony, everyone clamouring for her –

ALEXA. Take a moment while running to examine yourself. How do you feel?

FIONA. I feel trapped. I no longer know myself. Who am I, and who am I trying to be? The pressure to be so many things, all the time, to different people is so intense that at times I feel

I could shatter at the slightest touch. I am a mother. I am
a professional. I am a friend. I am a lover. I am an ex-wife.
I am a consumer. I am all of these things, and none. Yet I feel
the need to be all of them all the time. Everything I say and
do is played back to me in real time, judged, silently and
vocally. I am strong. I am beautiful. I am good. I am in
control of everything, and yet –

She turns and sees SCROOGE *through the glass –
part-reflection, part-ghost.*

SCROOGE. I do not feel –

FIONA. In control –

SCROOGE. I feel controlled by –

FIONA. A system I did not invent, which prizes growth and
profit and acquisition above all else.

SCROOGE. And requires us to perform for these gods
constantly –

FIONA. Obliging our every move, our every look to be
eternally judged –

SCROOGE. Culminating in this annual festival of getting and
spending.

FIONA. The pressure to make it perfect increasing year by
year –

SCROOGE. Not to mention the cost –

FIONA. Financial, physical, emotional –

SCROOGE. When, in fact, all we want –

FIONA. What Christmas is truly about –

SCROOGE. Should always have been about –

FIONA. Is that all we want –

SCROOGE. Have only ever wanted –

They 'touch' hands through the glass.

FIONA. Is to love.

SCROOGE. And to be loved.

FIONA. Not for what we are –

SCROOGE. But who.

> FUTURE *burns with light before disappearing.* SCROOGE *and* FIONA *spin around, the office revolving and fragmenting around them.*

COMPANY (*softly*). And when in scenes of glory
We sing the new, new song
'Twill be the old, old story
That we have loved so long!
'Twill be the old, old story
That we have loved so long!

Scene Seven

And we are back in SCROOGE*'s bedroom.*

Dawn is breaking – Christmas dawn.

MEAGRE. The bedpost was her own. The bed was her own, the room was her own, and quite gloriously, and best of all, the time was her own.

WANT. Oh. Finally. Can we curl up and go to sleep now? I'm so tired.

IGNORANCE. Not yet, sister. Nearly, though.

> *The great bell sounds a sudden, golden, echoing Christmas peal, sending* SCROOGE *bolt upright.*

SCROOGE. Where am I? Who am I? Am I really here, now, in this moment?

She sneezes!

I live! I can live again. I live in the past, the present, and the future, and it will be different! The spirit of all three shall strive within me. Look – the bed curtains! The bed curtains are still here!

She starts bouncing up and down on the bed.

The bed curtains are here! I'm not dead! The bed curtains haven't been pawned! The bed curtains –

She looks at them for a moment, and rips them down.

(*To audience.*) What are you staring at? I never liked them anyway. Let us throw away the shadows of my life. All of them! Look, that was the candle that became Christmas Past… that the robe the giant of Christmas Present… and those haunted sheets seem to have gone for good, thank God. Your ghosts are banished, Jacob Marley, and so are you. Free, free at last! I will be free. Everyone can be free!

She rips off her nightdress, revealing extravagant Victorian underwear, and skips about the stage.

MEAGRE. She frisked, she gambolled, she hallooed and she laughed – for someone who had not laughed in a very long time, it was the most splendid of laughs.

SCROOGE. I don't know what to do! I am as light as a feather, happy as an angel and merry as a schoolgirl… Merry Christmas! Merry Christmas, everybody!

She waits for a response from the audience.

I said Merry Christmas, everybody!

Keeps going till they reply.

And Happy New Year! Hanukkah Sameach! Wishing you all a belated Happy Diwali! Eid Mubarak! Happy Holidays! Happy hashtag National-Bring-Your-Cat-to-Work-Day! Oh my goodness, I have to give presents… presents… what have we got?

Rummages amongst her belongings.

An old gruel saucepan? With nothing in it? No, that's not enough... Do you want these bed curtains? Seriously? (*Improvising.*) They'll only end up on eBay. Come on, I don't want to throw them away, we know how bad that is for the environment, go on, Wilton's will get done by the council – again... (*Etc.*)

The audience are persuaded to take the curtains, which are passed over their heads.

But that's not enough...

MEAGRE. She ran out into the street. No fog, no mist, clear, bright, jovial, stirring, cold, piping for the blood to dance to; golden sunlight; heavenly sky, sweet air, fresh bells! It was glorious, even if I say so, as a cat who never thinks anything is glorious. Glorious!

SCROOGE. Yoohoo, little children, with a cat, what day is it?

IGNORANCE. Yer what?

SCROOGE. The day! What day of the year is it today?

WANT. It's Christmas Day, yer mad old bint.

SCROOGE. It's Christmas! It's only blooming Christmas! Those magical old spirits, they weren't half magical to do all that in one night!

MEAGRE. Even if to some of those watching it may have felt considerably longer.

SCROOGE. Right, kids! Do you know the butcher's on the corner, one street along?

IGNORANCE. Wait – this isn't gonna be something weird, is it?

SCROOGE. Weird? I can't think of anything less weird, than what I am about to ask you to do. This is the least weird thing anyone in history has ever asked some random passing children to do.

IGNORANCE. I knew it. It's going to be something weird.

SCROOGE. Do you know whether they've sold the prize turkey that was hanging there?

IGNORANCE. Told you.

WANT. The one as big as me?

SCROOGE. That's the one! Go and buy it for me, will you?

WANT. She has totally lost the plot.

SCROOGE. You're right! I have! And it's wonderful!

She empties a sack of coins in their general direction in a shower.

Then deliver it to the Cratchits! And… keep the change!

COMPANY (*sings*). O come, all ye faithful
Joyful and triumphant
O come ye, o come ye to Bethlehem
Come and behold Him
Born the King of Angels!

As they sing, SCROOGE's bedroom melts away, a curtain of brightly coloured chains rises up. Only these are paper chains.

Scene Eight

SCROOGE *dances into the street as the carol continues, and the paper chains continue to rise.*

COMPANY (*sings*). O come, let us adore Him
O come, let us adore Him
O come, let us adore Him
Christ the Lord!

She runs into MR BULLABY.

SCROOGE. My dear sir, please forgive me! It's Mr Bullaby, isn't it?

BULLABY. Indeed it is, Miss Scrooge.

SCROOGE. The fellow raising money for the evangelical school for young ladies?

BULLABY. That's right. I thought –

SCROOGE. Merry Christmas to you, sir, for what you thought was wrong! What I thought was wrong! What we all thought was wrong! Tell me, are you still accepting donations?

BULLABY. Of course we are! Are you all right, Miss Scrooge? Has something happened?

SCROOGE. Only the most wonderful thing in the world. I have seen the truth. I have felt the love. How much do you want?

BULLABY. I don't know, I mean – how much do you want to give?

SCROOGE. I mean for the school; how much do you want for the school?

BULLABY. But the school is not for sale, we are still raising funds –

SCROOGE. Name your price. Come on, how much?

BULLABY. Madam, I am not sure I made myself clear. My Home for Fallen Young Ladies is –

SCROOGE (*showing him bulging sack of coins*). How about this? Will that do it?

BULLABY. – for sale to the right buyer… but are you quite sure?

SCROOGE. As sure as I've ever been about anything. There you go! Sold!

She exchanges the sack and seals the sale with a shake.

BULLABY. Will you continue our noble mission?

SCROOGE. Over my dead body! Wave goodbye to Fallen Young Ladies and say hello to Fan Scrooge's School for Independent and Empowered Women!

BULLABY. But we mustn't empower them! They have fallen!

SCROOGE. And I shall raise them up! To the sky! Now, Mr Bullaby, I must bid you good day, for I am most grievously late already –

BULLABY. What on earth for?

SCROOGE. For Christmas lunch, what do you think?

And she whirls on to FREDERICA*'s door, which she raps at sharply.*

Scene Nine

FREDERICA*'s home.*

The paper chains continue to rise!

FREDERICA *opens the door uncertainly, with* FROU-FROU.

FREDERICA. Oh – Aunt Scrooge!

SCROOGE. Merry Christmas, dear niece!

FROU-FROU (*sings*). And a Happy New Year!

FREDERICA. Merry Christmas to you too, dear Aunt! Is everything all right? (*Notices bloomers.*) You look… different.

SCROOGE. Different? You have no idea how different! Now yesterday, you mentioned something about dinner –

FREDERICA. Oh yes, but of course! We've only just started… I'm sure Neville and Topper won't mind –

SCROOGE. – if they're not invited? That is so terribly obliging of them, because you ALONE are my guest, now come along my dear, forget your coat, we haven't a moment to lose!

FREDERICA. But what will the men say?

SCROOGE. Who cares! Good luck to them!

FREDERICA. Can I bring Frou-Frou?

SCROOGE. I mean, you will anyway, right?

FROU-FROU (*looking back indoors at* NEVILLE *and* TOPPER). Don't leave me with them!

SCROOGE. Then make haste, niece, make haste!

She drags FREDERICA *out –*

FREDERICA. But where are we going?

SCROOGE. To the best Christmas party in the world!

COMPANY (*sings*). O come, all ye faithful
O come, all ye faithful

O come, all ye faithful to Bethlehem
O come, all ye faithful
O come, all ye faithful
O come, all ye faithful to Bethlehem.

They have arrived at the CRATCHITS' *and the paper chains are fully up.* SCROOGE *raps at the door.*

Scene Ten

BOB CRATCHIT *opens the door –*

CRATCHIT. Miss Scrooge! (*Sees her bloomers.*) *Miss Scrooge!!!*

SCROOGE (*as her former self*). Cratchit. Now did I tell you that you could take Christmas off?

CRATCHIT. Begging your pardon, ma'am, but you did –

SCROOGE. That was very remiss of me.

CRATCHIT. How so?

SCROOGE. Because I wish for you to take not just Christmas, but the rest of your life off!

CRATCHIT. Come again?

SCROOGE. A salary for life, you heard me. It will make up for all those times I made you work overtime without adequate pay.

CRATCHIT. I don't mean to be rude, but are you quite all right in the head?

SCROOGE. Not really – now, are you going to stand there all day gawping like a goldfish, or are you going to let us in?

CRATCHIT. Us?

SCROOGE. My niece Frederica of course! I believe you've met.

FROU-FROU *barks loudly.*

And Frou-Frou. We're all coming for Christmas dinner.

They charge in, MRS CRATCHIT *and* TINY TIM *around the same table as before, they all stand in embarrassment –*

MRS CRATCHIT. Begging your pardon, ma'am, only we wasn't expecting company –

SCROOGE. Less of the 'ma'am' if you don't mind. Please call me Fan.

MRS CRATCHIT. Ann Cratchit at your service, Fan.

SCROOGE. Ann! Splendid! Ann – would you like a job?

ANN. I have a job, at the hat factory –

SCROOGE. A different job, then!

ANN. What kind of different?

SCROOGE. I thought perhaps one that doesn't break your back and your fingers for a start...

ANN. Then there's the housework, looking after Tiny Tim –

SCROOGE. It's all right, Bob's going to take all that on from now, aren't you, Bob?

BOB. I am?

SCROOGE. I read that book of yours, Bob. The Engels one with the funny name?

BOB. *The Condition of the Working Class in England*?

SCROOGE. That's the one. A condition we are going to change, together. Come the New Year, I am putting Marley and Scrooge on the market. Then we're going to run the school I just bought from Mr Bullaby. And with the proceeds from the company sale, I'm going to give you enough money to stay at home more –

BOB. At home?

SCROOGE. Don't you like looking after Tiny Tim?

BOB. I love nothing more in the world!

SCROOGE. Then why not do it forever? But first, can you run some final errands for me?

BOB. It will be my pleasure.

SCROOGE. Get yourself down to the Dorsets –

BOB. They say they can't pay.

SCROOGE. And nor shall they! Their debt is cancelled, and I want you to bring them here to lunch.

CRATCHIT *goes*.

Now, Tiny Tim, where are you there?

TINY TIM. I am here, ma'am.

SCROOGE. And how do you feel this Christmas morning?

TINY TIM. I always feel happy on Christmas Day.

SCROOGE. Do you promise not to die?

TINY TIM. I don't know if anyone can promise that.

SCROOGE. But do you promise to live a good and long and happy life?

TINY TIM. I shall try!

ANN. What will become of me? With Tim and Bob at home all the time? What will I do with myself?

SCROOGE. Ann, I'll tell you. How are you fixed for walking?

ANN. I go far enough each day – to the well, the grocer's, the market and more –

SCROOGE. Can you bear to walk a few miles further?

ANN. Where to?

SCROOGE. Into the future! I'm going to ask you to march with me. And perhaps even Frederica and Frou-Frou too?

She unfurls a suffragette banner reading:

'DEEDS NOT WORDS'.

ANN. But what are we marching for?

SCROOGE. The same thing people have always marched for, and always will. Freedom! And Love!

ANN. You mean I am free?

SCROOGE. To take on the world, Ann Cratchit, yes, by Christmas, you are!

ANN. That's very kind of you, Fan, but not on an empty stomach. Now if you'll excuse me – I'd better see to the dinner to make sure we have enough for everyone –

ANN *leaves to check the kitchen supplies.*

SCROOGE (*calling after her*). You don't need to worry! I already sent ahead. Children!

IGNORANCE *and* WANT *bring on the* TURKEY (*the same one from the* BEAU *Christmas scene*).

Wonderful, children! Except... (*Peering at bird.*) have I seen you before?

TURKEY (*shaking head*). Nope. Gobble Gobble.

SCROOGE. Are you sure? It's just that...

TURKEY. Yeah, yeah, we all look the same. Absolutely typical, to be honest. I get it all the time.

IGNORANCE. Look, mate, you might want to wind your neck in before it gets chopped off.

TURKEY. Easy! I'm only a turkey. Gobble gobble!

SCROOGE. I knew it! You really are a glutton for punishment, aren't you?

TURKEY. Are you kidding? Turkeys *love* Christmas! It always gets my vote.

SCROOGE. Then so it should! Please, my dear bird, be our honoured guest instead –

TURKEY. Don't mind if I do... but just so you know, I don't do dairy or carbs, hope that won't be a problem...

SCROOGE. Of course not. I'm sure we can make do without.

IGNORANCE. What, no turkey? At Christmas!!

SCROOGE. Oh stuff it. I'm going vegan. Might as well, everyone else has.

WANT. Then with that, there was nothing left for anyone to say, but –

SCROOGE *and* COMPANY. MERRY CHRISTMAS, EVERYONE!

IGNORANCE. Scrooge was better than her word. She did it all, and infinitely more, and to all the Cratchits was like a second mother. She became as good a friend to the working people, especially women and children, as this good old city had ever known.

MEAGRE. And animals of every kind!

WANT. Some people laughed to see the alteration in her, like her former lover Beau, but she let them laugh and little heeded them, for she knew that nothing good had ever happened in this world which people had not laughed at to begin with.

The music begins for our final hymn –

MEAGRE. She never saw another ghost again as long as she lived, but it was always said that she knew how to keep Christmas well, if anyone alive knew the secret of that. Her guiding principles always were truth, kindness and love.

IGNORANCE. What happened to us then?

WANT. We're still here, brother.

IGNORANCE. We're not, are we?

WANT. In the street, at yer winder, outside yer door. (*To audience*.) You never even noticed.

IGNORANCE. What, even though she mended her ways?

WANT. Even though.

IGNORANCE. So what now?

MEAGRE. Tell everyone, children. Tell them your story, and never stop telling them until they hear it.

Everyone joins in.

COMPANY (*sings*). I love to tell the story
    For those who know it best
    Seem hungering and thirsting
    To hear it like the rest!

IGNORANCE. May that truly be said of us and all of us.

WANT. And so as Tiny Tim observed –

MEAGRE. For many a Christmas after that –

TINY TIM. God bless us, every one!

COMPANY. And when in scenes of glory
    We sing the new, new song
    'Twill be the old, old story
    That we have loved so long!
    'Twill be the old, old story
    That we have loved so long!

End.

www.nickhernbooks.co.uk

 facebook.com/nickhernbooks

twitter.com/nickhernbooks